THE EAST EDGE

Chris McCabe's work crosses artforms and genres including poetry, fiction, non-fiction, drama and visual art. His work has been shortlisted for the Ted Hughes Award and the Republic of Consciousness Prize. His latest poetry collection, *The Triumph of Cancer*, was a Poetry Book Society Recommendation. He is the editor of *Poems from the Edge of Extinction: An Anthology of Poetry in Endangered Languages*. His first novel, *Dedalus*, is a sequel to *Ulysses*, his second, *Mud*, a version of the legend of Orpheus and Eurydice set underneath Hampstead Heath. He works as the National Poetry Librarian at Southbank Centre's National Poetry Library.

## ALSO BY CHRIS MCCABE

CREATIVE NON-FICTION

*In the Catacombs: A Summer Among the Dead Poets of West
    Norwood Cemetery* (Penned in the Margins, 2014)
*Real South Bank* (Seren, 2016)
*Cenotaph South: Mapping the Lost Poets of Nunhead Cemetery*
    (Penned in the Margins, 2016)

FICTION

*Dedalus* (Henningham Family Press, 2018)
*Mud* (Henningham Family Press, 2019)

POETRY

*The Hutton Inquiry* (Salt Publishing, 2005)
*Zeppelins* (Salt Publishing, 2008)
*THE RESTRUCTURE* (Salt Publishing, 2012)
*Speculatrix* (Penned in the Margins, 2014)
*The Triumph of Cancer* (Penned in the Margins, 2018)

AS EDITOR

*The New Concrete: Visual Poetry in the 21$^{st}$ Century,*
    with Victoria Bean (Hayward Publishing, 2015)
*Poems from the Edge of Extinction: An Anthology of Poetry in Endangered
    Languages* (Chambers, 2019)

# The East Edge

## Nightwalks with the Dead Poets
## of Tower Hamlets

## CHRIS MCCABE

*with photographs by Harpreet Kalsi*

Penned in the Margins
LONDON

PUBLISHED BY PENNED IN THE MARGINS
Toynbee Studios, 28 Commercial Street, London E1 6AB
www.pennedinthemargins.co.uk

First published in 2019

Printed in the United Kingdom by CPI Group

ISBN
978-1-908058-68-3

The author acknowledges the support of Arts Council England

CONTENTS

# The East Edge

# Nightwalks with the Dead Poets of Tower Hamlets

*The City is of Night; perchance of Death*
*But certainly of Night.*

B.V. THOMSON, *THE CITY OF DREADFUL NIGHT* (1874)

# The Terrors of the Night
## —— ENTERING THE CEMETERY

*And since he cannot spend and use aright*
*The little time here given him in trust,*
*But wasteth it in weary undelight*
*Of foolish toil and trouble, strife and lust,*
*He naturally claimeth to inherit*
*The everlasting Future, that his merit*
*May have full scope; as surely is most just.*

B.V. THOMSON, *THE CITY OF DREADFUL NIGHT*

I HAVE CROSSED THE RIVER and arrive in east London at night. I am trawling the Magnificent Seven to find a great lost poet and have entered the eastern fringe of the city, the realm of the Roman Necropolis. If I'd have arrived at any of the other seven cemeteries at this hour, I'd be too late — a bellman or groundsman would have locked the gates. Tower Hamlets Cemetery Park is the only one to remain open after dark.

Night starts early in the East End. In November, darkness starts to fall at 4pm. A momentary twilight takes place when the lights in the high-rise blocks glister with the last of the sun. The

Southern Grove entrance is closed so I walk around the outside walls of the Cemetery to find an entrance. Where the surrounding wall of the cemetery ends, the boundary is continued with terraced houses. Inside one is an active green light — the colour of a bluebottle's eye — blinking behind thick glass. I hear a train running nearby. Then a woman's high heels. The wind is pushing dead leaves through the gutter. A siren. A man flies past me on a bicycle, the red light flashing behind him like the eye of a Cyclops. This is London, even this. The commute takes place above the dead.

From the medieval period until the 19th century, various institutions of power have imposed restrictions on the citizens of London after dark. The walled City of London would close its gates, leaving malcontents locked out on the other side. These days the grounds of the Cemetery Park are open to all through the night. This land belongs to the community. I follow the dogleg of Ropery Street, past a BUILDERS merchants. The old east London trades still echo on here. Building. Plumbing. Ironmongery. Ropery Street is named after the rope-making industry that was here before the cemetery.

In *Nightwalking: A Nocturnal History of London*, Matthew Beaumont argues for a distinction between the Noctambulant, the one who is out walking with a purpose, and the Noctavigant, the one who walks with criminal intent. For a long period of London's history, just to be outdoors at night was to be considered criminal. This was particularly the case for the working class, for whom there is always another set of rules. Who in authority believes that the poor just pop out for a stroll, or take a walk to look at the moon?

Who am I then: Noctambulant or Noctavigant? Two years before the cemetery was opened, the Metropolitan Police Act of 1839 was passed, effectively criminalising those out in the city after dark. But the cemetery I'm walking towards has become a space impossible to control with light or truncheon. No Peelers on patrol. 'The Annoyance of the Inhabitants or Passengers' doesn't count here, and the dead don't care.

The frosted glass windows of the Victorian terraces are lit from within; illuminated images project like a Symbolist poem. A deep red flower. Green swans. Signs sent out from the living on the other side. One house has attached a candle holder to the left of the door as if anticipating a shroud of Whitechapel fog. Marigolds are curling in hanging baskets like parsnip crisps. Then the past disappears as the road forks into a vista of high-rises, each lit with a spine of orange bulbs, and beyond them a crane — neon red — semaphoring to low-flying helicopters.

A creaking green gate opens towards the field at the back of the grounds on Bow Common Lane. Powered lights make the walk as safe as anywhere in central London — but only if you're at peace with being so close to a quarter of a million burials. The lit path comes to an end. A footway retained through common use, into the land of the dead. My shadow stretches ahead towards my destination. I reach the kissing gate into the cemetery grounds and enter; I am inside. I hear the sound of a pig squealing. Then a woman hissing. An owl flutters overhead. Except it's none of these things — unlikely anyway — only the amplification of imagination that happens in graveyards. In *The Terrors of the Night* (1594), a book that I've carried about with me for years, Thomas Nashe wrote:

> 'If in the dead of the night there be any rumbling, knocking or disturbance near us, we straight dream of wars or of thunder. If a dog howl, we suppose we are transported into hell, where we hear the complaint of damned ghosts. If our heads lie double or uneasy, we imagine all heaven with our shoulders, like Atlas. If we be troubled with too many clothes, then we suppose the night mare rides us.'

I keep walking, glancing at the time on my phone. It's only just gone 5pm. Millions of Londoners are finishing work and boarding the Tube, and here I am, sweating in the cold — reaching for a tree to stay on my feet in a tangle of branches and long grass.

Then I'm lost. I ask two people who are sitting on a bench if I'm in the cemetery. They stare at me. "Graveyard?" I ask. They come alive, the tip-ends of their cigarettes bobbing like lights on a ship. "Straight ahead," one of them says. "Follow the path; put your light on so you can see." 'In the dead of night,' writes Matthew Beaumont, 'the underside of London might be found, and a secret self silently fostered.'

Three teenagers run in from the gates behind me, giggling. A minute later they're running back out. One says: "I want to do this but I'm too scared." This is one of the few central London locations without streetlights. The cemetery exists in an equilibrium between the citizens that frequent it, the law and the dead. Beaumont again: 'Nightwalking, it might be said, takes place in the realm of the unnight, a liminal zone between the waking and sleeping city, and between the waking and sleeping state of mind — even between the living and the dead.' If my mind is reeling so early in the evening, what will the cemetery reveal at 10pm, at midnight, in the early hours of morning? I feel like a swimmer who is about to complete their first length of a pool but is already thinking ahead to the Hellespont.

A train flies past overhead, like a horizontal version of one of the many tower blocks that colonnade the east London skyline. Someone is walking behind me with urgency, rattling keys. I speed up. Headstones begin to appear like the skyline of a far-off city. At this stage in my journey through the Magnificent Seven — the name given to the seven cemeteries built around London and opened between 1833 and 1841 — there's something homely about the graves, a familiarity that's come about through spending so many hours with the dead. The descent into the underworld plays tricks with the mind, but the underworld itself might just be a safe haven.

I've entered the necropolis, The City of Dreadful Night, to quote the title of B.V. Thomson's long poem. A light from the Hamlets Way side of the cemetery seems to twist and transforms into the shadow of an obelisk. If at night the dead were to reappear above ground, by dawn there would be no room for the living to leave their houses; so said Charles Dickens in 'Night Walks', written after experiencing a period of insomnia. With the population of London exploding from 865,000 in 1801 to almost nine million in 2019, the dead would win in a tug-of-war. I'm not even half-way through the Magnificent Seven and my own midlife is fluttering like a moth around an oil lamp. Roberto Bolano, documenter of Chile and Mexico after dark, writes in his epic *2666* that there are only two kinds of person out at night: those who are running out of time, and those with time to burn. I'm becoming familiar to the dead, a stranger to the living. I am moving through life with an ever-growing assembly line of overlooked poets, figures so marginal they curl up like the cuttings in the tray of a guillotine.

I stop beneath the bowing figure of a stone angel. Its wings momentarily appear like an overpacked rucksack. Harbinger of the eternal commute. As I walk forward it is dwarfed by the shadow of the Celtic cross next to it. Apartment windows flicker through branches. I wonder, perhaps, if electricity is sourced from the dead, an inversion of Galvinism (the biological contraction of muscle matter by an electric source used to activate Frankenstein's monster). Memorials race up to the sky. I'm lost in this ocean of night, enveloping folds of darkness that pull me further into the grounds. Somewhere inside a woman has lost her dog: "Abraham," she shouts. "Abrahaaaam!" A man passes, following the promise of his phone screen. Purpose. Plans. Appointments. When I walk out of the cemetery in a few hours, I'll join him on that mission, jump on a Tube, and become part of the tireless trade-off of lived hours for wage labour. I prefer it here, within touching distance of dead poets.

According to Meller and Parsons, by the start of the 20th century Tower Hamlets was distinct amongst London cemeteries:

'No other… had been allowed to grow wild for so long.' I think of Nunhead with its empire of vegetation and forests. I was so lost inside that landscape that only writing *Cenotaph South* could get me out of it. It's not so much the vegetation in Tower Hamlets that confuses as the criss-crossing paths which ask for decisions to be made on the hoof. There's nature here in abundance, with over 100 species of birds and, in spring and summer, butterflies. I can sense the creatures of winter tonight: urban foxes foraging for slugs, snaffling a bone.

A series of oddly shaped graves appears before me like a coven of hooded monks. As I move, they seem to move too. The Charterhouse graves are one of the strangest sights here and are distinct for their serrated, pointed designs. These graves house 200 brothers of Sutton's Hospital in the Charterhouse. Each grave contains the remains of six brothers. Dormitories extend into death, House Rules abolished. The memorials stand as a community, cut in the same uniform, united in their pilgrimage, marching into death together.

I scan my torch across the headstones and note the prevalence of nautical imagery. The mile or so walk down to the docks, across the Ratcliffe Highway, was one that many sailors did in reverse, after death; their bodies were carried across land, in coffins, on a tidal wave of living shoulders. Of the Magnificent

Seven, Brompton Cemetery might be closer to the river, but it is Tower Hamlets that is most *of* the river. I close my eyes and smell, through loamy earth, the water of the Thames. The cemetery holds the 23 people drowned in the paddle steamer *The Princess Alice*, which sunk in the Thames in 1871. Meller and Parsons list others claimed by river and sea, though not always as a result of the water itself. Captain Lusby was accidentally shot on board a ship in 1874. Peter Slader fell into the West India Dock in 1848. Death was never far away for the Victorian Londoner, but then neither was poetry, and the memorials of many of the dead are lineated with text that appear like haikus. My torch flashes across the memorial of Emma Simpkins.

She died at sea
of dysentry
on her passage to India 1854.

If she had died a year earlier this would have been in perfect end-rhyme. But death is never in end-rhyme; it's always resisted, on some level, by someone — either the afflicted themselves or their family. Poetry itself has formed a major part of the memorialisation of death here. In *Design for Death*, Barbara Jones describes how a bereaved family made a piano from chrysanthemums for their loved one, with a keyboard of scarlet carnations. A purple ribbon read 'Good Night Pop'. A eulogy was written on a sheet of paper.

> Around a piano we have
> Gathered through the years
> A legacy of happiness and
> Laughter that shines
> Through the tears

I've lost track of time. I check my phone but the battery has died. A far-off bell is ringing. Last orders? I've taken my first swim in the night cemetery. I make for a drink before the city locks me out.

# 𝔗𝔥𝔢 𝔇𝔦𝔰𝔢𝔪𝔟𝔬𝔡𝔦𝔢𝔡 𝔈𝔰𝔰𝔞𝔶

WILLIAM SPEAKS ————

'To seek to lay the ghost by wrapping it,' Henry James wrote of the death of his American cousin Minny, who died from tuberculosis when she was 24. The artist feeds on the loss until it transforms: *The Wings of the Dove*. 'By wrapping it... in the beauty and dignity of art.' James defined her death as the end of his youth and in this novel his mature style emerged: the pupa's little force explodes the case. To wrap the ghost and thereby to seek it. What solace for the artist in the loss of the flesh? Did James find a fair exchange in readership? All was not lost in his loss; a creation was born that was not there before.

*To seek. To wrap. To prove. To ghost.*

# Noctavigation by Daylight

*The city is not ruinous, although*
*Great ruins of an unremembered past,*
*With others of a few short years ago*
*More sad, are found within its precincts vast.*
B.V. THOMSON, *THE CITY OF DREADFUL NIGHT*

BEFORE LOSING MYSELF TOO DEEPLY in the cemetery, I've got a meeting with Manager Ken Greenway. I need a grounding by daylight so I can walk with a surer step here after dark.

It's hard to comprehend that Tower Hamlets Cemetery Park was once on the fringes of London. I arrive via Mile End station and walk straight into the morning commute. A five-lane gridlock of humans rushes along Mile End Road. Retro headphones provide half-halos. Wires hang from necks like stethoscopes. A man wearing red trousers fixes his perm. A woman with a grey cardigan and sports shoes sighs loudly. Londoners are accustomed to bearing the metaphysical static of the commute with complete impatience.

Needles of rain start to fall. Used cigarettes smoulder at the top of a bin. A map states, YOU ARE HERE, and shows a circle across the crossroads between Stepney and Bow. I zip my coat, pull up my hood, and walk against the flow. There's no mad rush to the graveyard this morning. Two children whisper like confidantes as they glide past on pink scooters. A woman clutches a copy of the morning's *Metro* to her chest, as if it has all the answers. I walk past the Rusty Bike, a heady combination of Thai restaurant and sports bar which is still in darkness after the night before. In the grounds of the flats along Mile End Road — facing the perfectly aligned Georgian terraces opposite — an apple has been placed on the top of a metal grille surrounding a sapling, fruitless tree. A tent has been erected inside a telephone booth to create a temporary private changing room; clothes have been placed on the outside frame, airing in the breeze.

I turn into Southern Grove. The obelisk of Canary Wharf winks, an electric pulse overlooking the dead of the East End. HSBC skywrites the clouds. A teddy bear is lying on the driver's seat of a parked Ford Focus. I pick up a fallen remembrance poppy — crisp and new — and place it on my jacket. All I need now is a sardonic rat and I could cameo in an Isaac Rosenberg poem.

The gates of Tower Hamlets Cemetery Park don't have the grandeur of West Norwood, the gothic flourishes of Nunhead or the Egyptian mystery of Abney Park — but they rise like the edges of portals into the 27 acres of the cemetery. Historically, there may have been less fear of the Resurrectionists here. The pattern on the gates of the cemetery could be symbolic of the labyrinthine paths inside. On Bow Common Lane, on the other side of the cemetery, is a chalk labyrinth. A jogger pushes onwards and through the opened gates, a bearded, lolling head plinthed on a Nike T-shirt. He disappears into a forest of sycamores, heading towards the maze.

I walk inside, past a man in a beanie hat carrying a mop and bucket. On the chalk board outside the Soanes Centre a question has been posed: *What's in the park today?* The answer follows: a male pheasant, a grey heron, firecrests and spindle berries. No poets listed. Here, in the heart of the East End, nature is thriving. It's easy to think that the proximity of death would have made the cemetery a place to be avoided, a Hades of human bones and decomposing bodies. This was certainly the case just 50 years after the cemetery opened. In her 1896 book, *London Burial Grounds*, Isabella Holmes described Bow Cemetery (as it was known then) as:

'a regular ocean of tombstones, many of which are lying about, apparently uncared for and unclaimed; in fact, most of the graves, except those at the edges of the walks, look utterly neglected, and parts of the ground are very untidy. It is situated in a densely-populated district.'

Images of the sea again come to mind. Sink or swim.

In the woodland before me, headstones are sliding earthwards. An angel seems to grab onto a crucifix to prevent the memorial from falling. Fresh flowers have been placed at the foot of a grave. The groundsmen are talking amongst each other. One says, "Welcome World War Three." The other responds with, "It wasn't the fact that she was a woman, it was the fact she was a Clinton." When the war breaks out, I think, the only safe place will be the cemetery. A man in a suit walks past me, blowing his nose; it's hard to know if this is due to mourning or man flu.

I spot Ken outside the Soanes Centre and wave across to him. We shake hands as he explains that today he's organising a group of volunteers from the Department of Transport who have come on a team building day. A dozen civil servants are holding wheelbarrows and spades. Tools of the trade. Ken introduces me and explains that I'm writing a book about the dead poets buried in the grounds. One of the volunteers asks Ken if he's ever seen a ghost? "No," he replies. "Ghosts are projections of the imagination." Then he recounts the story of a woman who told him one night that she'd seen the ghost of a woman in a wheelchair at the end of one of the paths.

If there's a perception that cemeteries are for the maudlin then Ken Greenway is the alchemist who radically alters it. He's the most ebullient guide I've found on my journey through the Magnificent Seven. The landscape gives him vigour, and why wouldn't it? As thousands pass the gates on their way to sedentary office jobs, Ken is outdoors, cultivating the earth, weeding, keeping a watch on the seasonal movements of nature. His cheeks are flushed with the good health that comes from working in a role that doesn't require team-building away-days or enforced high-vis.

This isn't to say Ken isn't a natural organiser. He's got today's volunteers pulling out cow parsley to increase the biodiversity of the earth beneath. I take a photograph of the group as they work — rare evidence of civil servants breaking into a sweat. Google Sheets replaced with the trellis-work of the May sun. Ken points out the flowers that are just over the bank in front of us. Huge plants loll like triffids. "That's the giant hogweed," he says, "the one the *Daily Telegraph* like to write obsessively about." The hogweed is phototoxic, can cause a severe sunburn reaction on the skin and is apparently out to kill us all. I make a note for my return visit; sunburn after dark won't bring me any closer to the dead poets I'm looking for.

Ken leaves the civil servants to bake in the sun and leads me further in. As we walk I ask him about the cemetery's relationship with the night. "There was all kinds of silliness going on at night," he says. "People would get locked in. The Parks Department wouldn't go around and check if there were people here, but even if they did you couldn't see them." Ken steers us towards an area of common graves and explains the situation now. "We're not locked in... the main gates get closed, but there are six kissing gates that never lock. So the park's always open in that sense. This has made the site safer because when we were locked — it was still a locked site when I came in 2002 — people had put car jacks in the railings to create permanent access points." It was then Ken that suggested to the council that things might work better if the cemetery was left open through the night. The council agreed to trial it and increased the number of gates from four to six. Kissing gates: a sentient hinge to the outside world.

There was a further benefit to closing the gates at night: it prevented people from bringing in motorbikes. Blood pulse accelerated by *memento mori*. Brake fluids lactating into the common graves.

Ken describes his approach to policing the cemetery as "interrupt and bother." Those bringing in bikes — teenage drinkers, junkies — are all approached in the same way and told to respect the place or leave. Ken says this as a matter of course, as if it's an inevitable part of working here, nothing to become angry about. He's thriving in his habitat: "My approach was to let them know I existed," he says. "Not be the nasty Parky, but present a persistent drip drip feed, like Chinese water torture... and it worked." The results are all around us today. The greenage we're walking through is abundant due to Ken's approach of micromanaging the climate. If the giant hogweed decides to get nasty I've got every faith that Ken could talk it back to the ground it rises from.

As we walk, I think of Jack London's *The People of the Abyss*, which documents the author's time spent undercover as an East End vagrant in 1902. London writes, 'And when I at last made into the East End, I was gratified to find that the fear of the crowd no longer haunted me. I had become a part of it. The vast and malodorous sea had welled up and over me, or I had slipped gently into it, and there was nothing fearsome about it.' London documents the phrase 'Carrying the Banner', which was an expression used by the East End poor to describe spending a night on the street. 'And I,' writes London, 'with the figurative emblem hoisted, went out to see what I could see.' Soon, I think, I'll be joining the past and present nightwalkers of the East End and carrying the banner myself.

Ken points down a path with graves on either side. "In my first fortnight here I had a burned-out car over there." Ken points to an open space of grassland between memorials and I picture a character from a Ballard novel raising the stakes on their auto-mania by racing bonnet-first into a row of graves. The crash-fetishists have gone now; with the introduction of the kissing gates no vehicles can get into the cemetery. "We are in London," Ken says, "you can never say never, but we talk to the police and they say they virtually get no crime reported here. This might not work for all of the Magnificent Seven, but staying unlocked of a night works for us."

There is a sense in which Ken has absorbed some of the characteristics of the landscape itself. He carries a peaceable acceptance of nature's tooth and claw, of the inevitability of dying. There's such a flourishing of plants, insects and birds here that the landscape must, in turn, have benefitted from Ken's approach of closely watching nature, cutting back in some places, and allowing for growth in others. There's depth to the greenness here — the inverse of the dusty pavements of Mile End Road.

With the support of his colleagues, volunteers and the Friends who employ him, Ken has shaped Tower Hamlets Cemetery Park into the most gregarious of the Magnificent Seven. His instinct is right: the dead lie neglected without the living. He tells me how, at a meeting of the Magnificent Seven cemeteries, it was observed that Tower Hamlets was the only one with a website that actually included photographs of *living* people. Ken's approach is to ensure that the cemetery reaches people on the level of what they want, not what those in power *think* they should want. His experience is that most people visit urban cemeteries to make contact with nature; an interest in architecture and memorials comes after. Ken's approach is at the cutting edge of cemetery management: "You've got to throw your gates open and not be so precious about things," he says. "The heritage can come when people get to know the space." It's then that Ken slips a poem in — he does this so subtly it would be easy to miss. "Most people feel it's not their history because they're not originally form around here, it's not immediately theirs. *Swap tower blocks for trees / And city noise for birds and bees.*"

I ask Ken about the catacombs that were here and he points to the spot where the volunteers are currently ripping out the cow parsley: "Council in the 1960s," he says. "The catacombs were collapsed and the Anglican chapel was probably pushed into them. We know now that the catacombs were probably seen as a bit European. People think that Brexit makes European scepticism a new thing, but the Victorians absolutely had an issue with the continent. The catacombs weren't very popular. I've spoken to people in here who remember calling the police because kids were down there rummaging around in them. The catacombs were very small here and even the chapel would only seat about forty."

Tower Hamlets Cemetery Park also had a Dissenters Chapel with catacombs underneath it. The area where this stood is currently marked out with wooden seats, in the octagonal shape of the chapel itself. Although there was historically a Dissenters' burial ground on the north side of the cemetery — in what is now known as Round Glade — religious non-conformers were also buried in other spaces. This is a very different approach to other cemeteries, in which these areas were clearly demarcated from Anglican grounds. Ken points along another path and tells me about a grave stamped with A.O.F. — the Ancient Order of Foresters. What sounds like a sect to defend London's Great North Wood was actually a precursor to the Freemasons and was open to anyone with a belief in a Creator. The organisation still exists today as the Foresters Friendly Society and boasts 75,000 members. I ask Ken about the poets buried here. He gives me the name of Diane Kendall, the volunteer in charge of heritage. She should be able to put me on the right track, he says — the track, I hope, to the East End's version of Parnassus.

Ken's got to get back to the civil servants before they dig up something they shouldn't, but I can't let him go without bringing him back to the cemetery at night. I tell him I'm thinking a lot about how the cemetery changes after dark and ask for his perspective. "Obviously there are no street lights here so you get a real sense of darkness in the city. There is light pollution, so it's never completely darkness. It just feels really peaceful. We do guided walks, moth walks, bat walks... I really like it. Maybe because it's a cemetery it creates a feeling amongst the group of being together. You can see that in the way people interact with each other. I find it really exciting here of a night, especially on a full moon."

As we're looking along the Southern Grove wall, Ken recognises a woman staring at a row of graves. He introduces me to Rachel Kolsky, London Blue Badge Tourist Guide. She is preparing to give a private tour of the cemetery next week. She's looking for the grave of John Northey, famous for rescuing people from *The Princess Alice* in 1878. Rachel is in a state I fully recognise: the needle-holder in a shifting piñata of graves. "The graves can't move can they?" she asks Ken, slightly exasperated. Northey has disappeared. As if the seaman had just got up and walked.

Rachel stands upright in a grey coat, with silver hair; she's nimble and somehow ageless — as if she moves too quickly for time to catch her. "I'm being rubbish," she says. "Where is he?" Ken has a good sense of where Northey is and walks Rachel further along the path in the direction of the Soanes Centre. "I always explain to my groups that cemeteries are so difficult," Rachel says. "It's the undergrowth! If you lose your bearings for a second you get lost! I've been here many times and now I can't find him... I'm so glad you're here Ken." Ken walks her forward as she asks, "Are we close? Is he here, Ken?"

Ken finds Northey and the world settles back into place. Rachel asks me if I'm working with Ken and he tells her I'm writing a book about the dead poets buried here. "Are you?!" she asks. "A *book* book, or a booklet?" The real thing I say, one with a spine. "Oh, so you concentrate on the poets!" I give her the background on my other books: *In the Catacombs*, about West Norwood Cemetery, and *Cenotaph South*, on Nunhead. The day job, I tell her, is collecting the *Collecteds* at the National Poetry Library. I ask if I can walk with her one time: "Oh, I don't know," she says, "I'm a rabbiter, aren't I, Ken? I rabbit on."

Ken really does need to get back to the civil servants, who may have dug up a body by now. But there's one last thing I need to ask him, an idea which has been mooted by my publisher and — tentative as I am to go there — a prospect that excites me. Is there scope to organise a performance here, for the public, one night? If I can find enough dead poets to write about, we could bring an actor and a musician to perform with me in the grounds. A multimedia *Inferno* for the Tower Hamlets dead. It's all night-sky gazing at the moment and I expect Ken might have logistics which close down the idea quickly, but he responds effusively. "Of course! Ask them to send me the details and we'll set up an Eventbrite page." All I need now are my dead poets.

I thank Ken and spend what might be my last hour absorbing the cemetery in the afternoon daylight. I pause in the sun and make a recording of the grounds. A woodpecker drills into a tree. A corvus rattles. A woodpigeon coos. And further off, as if calling from the past, a train whistles. What does day bring that the night takes away? Ease of sight. A more secure path. Safety? I feel reassured by Ken's words, but can I realistically find long lost dead poets in the darkness? And the idea of me performing something here, by night, is starting to shape into reality. I'm going to carry the banner, but what will my banner say? LIVING INVESTIGATOR SEEKS BODIES OF DEAD POETS. No, it's their *words* I want, and perhaps my performance will be the right method for broadcasting them as far as possible. The dark could blanket me in, shut out all other distractions. Close out everything but the words that link us together as poet and reader. Searcher and found. Walker and interned. Dead and living. I make a note to check the celestial chart. I want my poets by full moonlight.

§

WILLIAM SPEAKS ————

What solace in the beauty and dignity of art? A world of things
appears behind the taut wingspan of overstretched vellum. I
hold what I've written to the UV light & the Health & Safety
Officer says, "protect your face." A pregnant woman walks
with an ageing dog. The woman wears shades. Most of what
I write is pressed straight to digital, lifted, replaced, erased in
invisible space — but I will not abandon the notebook: like a
raft on land for the days of the flood. Here are marks pressed
on the page — so many of them — from which memory is
made. The transparencies mark the invisible folds of memory.
Did you really say we all live two lives?

*To hold. To stretch. To lift. To write.*

# Dusking the Day
## —— TRACKING DOWN WILLIAM MORRIS

*Yet in some necropolis you find*
  *Perchance one mourner to a thousand dead,*
*So there; worn faces that look deaf and blind*
  *Like tragic masks of stone.*

B.V. THOMSON, *THE CITY OF DREADFUL NIGHT*

THERE MAY BE SCANT EVIDENCE for buried poets here, but I've made some links thanks to Diane Kendall of the Friends group. Among the seven names I've been given are *four* Williams: Sherrard, Ivatts, Pearson and, the wildcard in the pack, William 'Spring' Onions. Onions was undoubtedly a poet, as was Salvation Army songwriter William J. Pearson, but the claims for Sherrard and Ivatts are tenuous. I've bought new batteries for my torch.

Today I'm here to explore the link between the death of Alfred Linnell and printer, poet and activist William Morris. Morris led the procession to Linnell's grave in 1887 and wrote a new poem for the occasion. I walk in gloom, over loam, and find the small, recently-erected memorial to Linnell on the path leading towards the Horse Chestnut Glade. It stands dwarfed by the elongated Victorian slabs around it. I tap the torch icon on my phone, shine it on the memorial; it is dun, squat and shaped like a toadstool, a half-risen loaf in an oven of bluebell and nettles.

My phone also furnishes me with the digitised version of Morris's pamphlet, *A Death Song*, which has spread from its original limited edition print run to become a luminous Socialist tract — still waiting for its overground moment in the culture. The design by Walter Crane shows a mounted policeman beating a man with a truncheon as the figures of Liberty and Justice try to intervene. Above Linnell's name, in bold caps, is the line, 'Sold for the benefit of Linnell's Orphans.' Mouths fed by letterpress. On Linnell's small grave is a quote from the Morris poem.

> Not one, not one, nor thousands must they slay
> But one and all if they would dusk the day

'Dusk the day' reads like a portent for my journey into the cemetery by night, it provides a kind of condensed yoking of extremes (dusk into day) and hints towards the kind of poetry I'd like to find here. Through the dark I see the outline of a jet black log next to the headstone; tiny flecks have broken away where a mastiff has had its teeth. A man walks past speaking into his phone: "Silence can be best but don't follow it up with a really boring question." I'm asking my own questions of the dead, awaiting their replies through the mild breeze of twilight.

Three weeks before Linnell's death, there had been demonstrations in London against unemployment and oppression in Ireland; events had turned violent after the police and troops had turned on the crowd with truncheons. Morris had been amongst the 10,000 protesters (along with George Bernard Shaw) and had made a speech from the back of a wagon. Morris talked of the 'good luck of being born respectable and rich' that allowed him to live away from 'the drink-steeped liquor shops and foul and degraded lodgings'. At the age of nearly 50 he became a Socialist. What he saw on the day of these attacks vindicated his mission to speak truth to power.

A week after this 'Bloody Sunday', Linnell, a young clerk who worked for a low wage copying out legal documents, joined another protest in Trafalgar Square and was knocked down by a 'restive' and 'bean-full' (Morris's words) police horse. The weight of the horse came down on his leg, shattering his thigh bone. Morris includes a statement from a witness, W. Edwin Davies, who describes finding Linnell in pain, calling out as if from his grave: "I'm a dead man, I'm a dead man." 'After the bone had been set,' Morris wrote in the account of Linnell's death that was published in the 'Death Song' pamphlet, 'the thigh had to be opened and a piece of bone taken out.' The pain was unbearable and although his nurse and his sister had expected him to recover, Linnell died of blood poisoning in a Charing Cross Hospital bed. A scent of sap rises and I look closely. Fronds of nipplewort stand upright — urgent flecks of yellow on the sleeping grass.

Morris describes how, after Linnell's death, 'the police were set to work to blacken the character of the man whom they had killed'. They had summoned a witness to say that Linnell 'was so drunk the night before his death he could not even make up his account'. The report stated that the police had acted with caution and were in no way culpable. There's a scuffling at the back of my heels, as if something has risen from the grave. I turn to find a black terrier in a red collar sniffing my leg. Satisfied that I'm not a tree, it huffs, and moves further into the dark centre of the cemetery.

Linnell is another case of a life of poverty ending in these burial grounds. His wife had already died and left him with children aged 10 and 12 years. The children were placed under the care of Linnell's brother-in-law. Having four children of his own, the brother-in-law put them in the workhouse. One of them had died there prior to Linnell's own demise. Morris was in no mood to sanctify Linnell, describing him as 'no popular hero.

He had been at one time somewhat unsteady... Linnell was in uncertain work, and he had many troubles.' The Socialists had planned a huge funeral service, with tens of thousands making the walk from the West End to the spot I'm standing on now.

The rain starts to fall and I shelter under the branches of a nearby tree. The rain that has been almost constant in London all summer, providing a soundtrack like the crackle left in a speaker system after a performance has finished. I sense the tremors of the crowd that had gathered here for Linnell's funeral, flushed from their walk, agitated with grief and political frustration. It was dusk by the time the crowds arrived; their speeches were read by lamplight, invectives of anger, sadness and resentment over misused power. A man and a woman in matching denim are now walking this ground with intent, their hands around cans of ready-made gin and tonic. Standing in the rain tonight it's easy to see how Morris made a Socialist utopia of Tower Hamlets Cemetery Park. He was a visionary of the night.

I hear what sounds like a ticking clock. A father and his son appear wearing hoodies, the teenager grinding the wheels on his bike. I look again at Morris's text on my phone; a rectangle of light glows up to my face. 'A Death Song' was sung as a lament for the dead at Linnell's funeral. Shadows under a nearby tree morph into the starched damp fabric of the Victorian mourners as I read it aloud, testing its strength as poem, but remembering it is song.

> What cometh here from west to east awending?
> And who are these, the marchers stern and slow?
> We bear the message that the rich are sending
> Aback to those who bade them wake and know.
>> Not one, not one, nor thousands must they slay,
>> But one and all if they would dusk the day.

> We asked them for a life of toilsome earning,
> They bade us bide their leisure for our bread;
> We craved to speak to tell our woeful learning:
> We come back speechless, bearing back our dead.
>> Not one, not one, nor thousands must they slay,
>> But one and all if they would dusk the day.

> They will not learn; they have no ears to hearken.
> They turn their faces from the eyes of fate;
> Their gay-lit halls shut out the skies that darken.
> But, lo! this dead man knocking at the gate.
>> Not one, not one, nor thousands must they slay,
>> But one and all if they would dusk the day.

> Here lies the sign that we shall break our prison;
> Amidst the storm he won a prisoner's rest;

But in the cloudy dawn the sun arisen
Brings us our day of work to win the best.
>> Not one, not one, nor thousands must they slay,
>> But one and all if they would dusk the day.

There is another question, lingering in the gloom, that I must address: what happened to Morris's reputation as poet? When we think of William Morris now we think of the snakeshead and trellises of his textiles, of Socialism and *News from Nowhere* — but it was for his poetry that he first became famous. In 1865 he started writing *The Earthly Paradise* in the offcuts of time left over from his printing business. This poetic tale recounts a journey by Nordic wanderers to find Paradise, arriving on an island inhabited by descendants of the ancient Greeks. In this clever re-versioning of Classical mythology, the two groups meet to tell each other stories. Nobody was more surprised than Morris to see the book become an instant bestseller. 'The talk of inspiration is sheer nonsense,' he wrote, 'it's a mere matter of craftsmanship.'

There's no doubt that Morris could write. His poem 'Love is Enough' shows a poet who could handle rhythm.

Love is enough: though the World be a-waning,
And the woods have no voice but the voice of complaining,

Though the sky be too dark for dim eyes to discover

The gold-cups and daisies fair blooming thereunder,

Though the hills be held shadows, and the sea a dark wonder

And this day draw a veil over all deeds pass'd over,

Yet their hands shall not tremble, their feet shall not falter;

The void shall not weary, the fear shall not alter

These lips and these eyes of the loved and the lover.

Morris broke from the hegemony of regular metre that constricted so many Victorian poets, writing instead in lines of irregular length which foreshadowed the work of the Modernists. There is confidence and authority in how Morris sets up an argument ('Love is enough') which is then resolved in the single sentence of the poem, ending with a return to the word 'lover'.

There's an echo of William Blake in Morris — Blake who also worked on his epic poems alongside the manufacture of printing plates. 'If a chap can't compose an epic poem while he's weaving a tapestry,' said Morris, 'he had better shut up, he'll never do any good at all.' Yet, as I've found before on my journey into these cemeteries, securing popularity in a poet's lifetime gives no reassurance of posterity. Morris was premature in drawing a sketch of himself, in 1883, sitting amongst the most famous poets of England — Swinburne, Browning, Arnold and Tennyson —

receiving laureate wreaths from the muse. Morris depicts himself close to the earth, holding a clump of daisies, symbolising his work with inks. He drew this picture for the cover of the anthology *English Living Poets*, little realising that cultural memory is unforgiving when it comes to a poet's legacy. Sales don't transfer to posterity. Who remembers now that Morris was so famous as a poet that he was offered the Laureateship in 1891 and turned it down for political reasons? (But then who remembers Alfred Austin, who accepted the post in his place?) When I studied English Literature at university in the 1990s, Morris was nowhere to be seen on the syllabus. If you dig through enough anthologies, a rootstalk or two can be found. Christopher Ricks gives Morris two pages in *The New Oxford Book of Victorian Verse*, a passing footnote in comparison to Arnold (10 pages), Swinburne (16), Browning (54) and Tennyson (47). But it is still a place in the literary canon, and one I suspect the lost poets buried here in Tower Hamlets Cemetery Park would crave.

I look back at Linnell's resting place and shine my torch to capture the detail. The grave next to Linnell's lies collapsed flat and is coated in moss like the baize of a snooker table. In the land behind them more graves stare back like depleted wanderers, waiting for benefaction. I look at one of them more closely, as if it might hold some clue to the alchemy that activates the work of

poets after their death. The stone urn on the grave of Ebenezer
Caleb Shepherd could be either half empty — or half full — and
it's too dark now to read the text.

§

In a café in the ancient park I watch October spread itself across the field. Crows patrol the pathways & tables. Umber leaves fly with such force. I am behind glass as I write this. When the café attendant disappears behind the counter, a crow lands on the surface next to a basket of jams. He shoes it away with a flailing hand. Preschool children run through the leaves, dogs crouch to shit, a woman sits on a bench to text. Soon my sabbatical will end & the real work will begin. Or is this, in fact, the real work? A toddler runs to the arm of the woman who lays down her phone; her text is suspended. A boy in a silver helmet gathers in sticks. The morning's work is done.

*To run. To work. To text. To end.*

# The Birth of Onions

*The City is of Night, but not of Sleep;*
  *There sweet sleep is not for the weary brain;*
*The pitiless hours like years and ages creep,*
  *A night seems termless hell.*

B.V. THOMSON, *THE CITY OF DREADFUL NIGHT*


JACK SPICER, POET of the San Francisco Renaissance, is remembered
for his final words: 'my vocabulary has done this to me'. Poets
have died with poetry as their only flag, the other end of it tied
around their necks. Villon killed a priest, was imprisoned — wrote
his testament — and disappeared from history. Rimbaud ruined
everyone who walked the trail with him, then left poetry behind
at the age of 21. Rosemary Tonks drifted through London's café
culture in the '60s, found religion, and retreated forever. In 1971
Lew Welch walked out of Gary Snyder's shack in the mountains
of California, leaving a suicide note and carrying a Smith &
Wesson .22 caliber revolver. His body was never found. Did he
combust into dry air? In all these cases it is the surviving poems
that endure. They stand in for their disappearances, for the quick
torture of their lives. Poets don't live once but — singing their

body electric — multiple times. They live whenever they're re-read. William 'Spring' Onions (1834?–1916), dead poet in the grounds of Tower Hamlets Cemetery Park, is yet to be published. But here is a poet who held court for much larger audiences than any living cult poet can hope to achieve.

His beginnings in life are unclear but he's as indigenous to the East End landscape as a disemboweled eel. Just like Dylan Thomas, he lived from his early teens in a near-permanent state of drunkenness. But unlike Thomas he had an inner Lazarus growing on the burst veins of his debauched flesh — Onions lived until twice the age of the later poet.

Onions was born in the 1830s to unknown parents. There are clues to the exact date and location of his birth, but none of them can be pinned to Onions with complete certainty. In 1835, the Parish Register of St George in the East records a William John Onions being born to a William and Ann Onions. However, it is more tempting to go with the alternative source of Stepney Workhouse; they held a record of a William Onions born around 1830. This record shows that the parents of this particular Onions were moved to Tooting Workhouse in December 1838; their children William and Ann were taken out of the workhouse by their grandfather on the 28th of that month, in the lag between the invisible goose and the non-starter of the New Year. Although a birth date of 1830 makes Onions older than he later claimed to be, this kind of confusion was common amongst the Victorian working class.

Onions was born into the acid spit of the East End and lived a hand-to-mouth struggle for the basics of food, warmth and sleep. This was the world that Jack London documented: 'A spawn of children clutter the slimy pavement, for all the world like tadpoles just turned frogs on the bottom of a dry pond.' For Onions, the workhouse was his maternity ward and his nursery; it provided him with the only structure he knew in life — until poetry rose up inside him like the black smoke of a censer. In *The People of the Abyss*, London shows a photograph of Poplar Workhouse at the start of the 20th century. A grungy alley leads to a rained-soaked slab of blackened bricks, a sordid Legoland of geometric walls and terraces lit by a single streetlight. To the homeless, Poplar Workhouse was the antithesis to the anarchy of the streets — behind the 42 identical grey windows there was water, food and safe lodgings — but when the undercover Jack London arrives to claim a bed for a night he's shocked by the conditions inside.

> A shirt was handed me—which I could not help but wonder how many other men had worn; and with a couple of blankets under my

arm I trudged off to the sleeping apartment. This was a long, narrow room, traversed by two low iron rails. Between these rails were stretched, not hammocks, but pieces of canvas, six feet long and less than two feet wide. These were the beds, and they were six inches apart and about eight inches above the floor. The chief difficulty was that the head was somewhat higher than the feet, which caused the body constantly to slip down. Being slung to the same rails, when one man moved, no matter how slightly, the rest were set rocking; and whenever I dozed somebody was sure to struggle back to the position from which he had slipped, and arouse me again.

In the 1840s Onions would have been emerging as a tadpole from the frogspawn of his childhood. As 'a voice' in Henry Mayhew's *London Labour and the London Poor* (1851) describes, 'If a poor boy gets to the workhouse he catches a fever, and is starved into the bargain.' Onions, however, was an amphibian, and perhaps through genetic disposition or sheer good luck could mutate from his liquid world into an unlikely old age.

The 1841 census shows a William Onions of six years of age as being resident in Whitechapel. There is then a long gap in the records until 1867 when the name again appears in the annals of Stepney Workhouse with the cryptic note, 'has a bad leg'. In the period between these two clues we know that Onions had discovered alcohol; if we fast forward to his obituary in *The*

*Monmouth Daily Atlas* we have an account of his first encounter with drink:

> More than three score and ten years ago a boy in the same East End made his way to the bar in a low public house and called for gin. When he went out it was with a lurching, staggering gait. The boy was William Onions and at 13 years old he was drunk. From that time on, for more than half a century, he never knew what it was to be sober.

What follows reads like a master plan in how to hit back at power with the body itself. As a teenager Onions pickled his insides so thoroughly with alcohol that his biggest threat was a lighted match. Onions hurtled headlong against institutional power, refusing to be silenced or made invisible — as if it were possible to knit his own physicality into the architecture of the East End.

Onions seems to have hit his stride by his mid-30s, but there's no reason to believe that this is anything other than a continuation of behaviours he'd already fine-tuned over the 20 years before. On 11th January 1868 he was discharged from Stepney Workhouse, only to be readmitted on the 28th with the following record: 'No Home – Unemployed – Destitute.' The long dashes and capitalised words ring out like a lost line of Emily

Dickinson. What follows is an accelerated series of admissions to the workhouse, with more discharges than a bubonic corpse. The pressure broke Onions and in October 1868 he was admitted to Colney Hatch Lunatic Asylum, between Barnet and Muswell Hill. The asylum still stands, a spear-tipped bell tower nestled between the colonnades of two imperious viewing posts. It is a building made to look out from. Its insides were built on an epic scale too, as if constructed to swallow thousands of inpatients. At its height it was known to have the longest corridor in Britain. It took over two hours to walk the entirety of its wards. For Onions, the individualist, this was no place to draw a crowd.

Colney Hatch proved to be a brief excursion out of east London for Onions. He was readmitted to Stepney Workhouse within two days of being released from the asylum. The note for a second admission on 15th December gave a description of where he was found, and how: 'Flower and Dean Street Destitute.' Flower and Dean Street was part of the Spitalfields Rookery, an inner-city slum where the impoverished lived in chronically overcrowded conditions amidst brothels and opium dens. In his 1854 book, *In Strange Company*, James Greenwood described it as 'perhaps the foulest and most dangerous street in the whole metropolis.' Two of Jack the Ripper's victims lived on this street. In 2014, criminologists at Queen Mary, University of London, used geographic profiling to locate the Ripper's home on Flower and Dean Street. Unpoliceable by night; a rook's nest overpowered by magpies. In this mapping of the criminal and destitute, Onions can be found at the epicentre of Victorian vice.

The bleakest years of Onions' life followed. In 1874 he was sentenced by the Central Criminal Court to a year's imprisonment for manslaughter. There is no record of what happened in this incident and no record of the man who died through Onion's negligence. Until he gave up alcohol at the turn of the century, almost the whole of Onions' life was spent in the red mist and curling fumes of drink-fuelled rage. Three gin-soaked rags to the wind, he was a fading ghost with a swinging bladder of porter.

A curious appearance of a William Onions can be found in the register of the workhouse in Selby, Yorkshire, in 1881. His age was given as 45 which roughly aligns with the birth date of William 'Spring' Onions. As with so many of the East End poor, it is worth repeating that Onions may have been unsure of his own age. If he had known it at some earlier point in life, then the quick acceleration of the years — lived between alcoholic blackout and the workhouse — would have made it difficult to keep count.

As later accounts of his statements in court show, Onions repeatedly talked of going outside of London as a curative to the trouble he caused the East End police; as such, there is good reason to believe that this is the same William Onions. On this occasion he gave his profession as 'Sugar Maker'. This switch into the fantastical gives us a glimpse of Onions the stifled poet, spinning together words for the fun of it, doing what all poets do in offering a version of himself that better suited his tortured imaginary. This is Onions as he should have been, a crystalliser of sweetened consumables, whose name would brighten up the face of every child. Not the sour breath that comes from mixing hard liquor with black bread. Onions had already achieved a notoriety that would have solidified a legacy as a criminal, but no one — least of all him — could have foreseen the strange turns his life would take.

§

WILLIAM SPEAKS ————

Then I'm astonished by the invention of a coffin emoticon.
What uses does this have? A friend tweets: 'I've used this to
describe hangovers, to document my love life, and for texting
bad film synopses.' The mind is telepathic, forces itself to
claim unresolved futures. Out in the field a toddler dressed
in red runs amidst the crows, a flame in the coals. Autumn is
the season when nature speaks. I walk across the underground
river where it surfaces from its underground flumes. Keats'
'season of... mellow fruitfulness' was the ripening of his death;
he made a still life from his living flesh. A boy called Max flies
past on a scooter bike.

*To tweet. To find. To flesh. To love.*

# Depart

*Although lamps burn along the silent streets,*
   *Even when moonlight silvers empty squares*
*The dark holds countless lanes and close retreats.*

B.V. THOMSON, *THE CITY OF DREADFUL NIGHT*

THE PLANS TO CREATE A PERFORMANCE in Tower Hamlets Cemetery Park are becoming real. I'm here with my publisher and live literature producer, Tom Chivers, to see what might be possible. We've got tickets for *Depart*, a site-specific dance performance created by LIFT for Spitalfields Festival, promising to 'seduce you down a path punctuated by unexpected encounters as you weave through the space between life and death.' I wonder if the dead poets will appear to cut some shapes on the dancefloor of the necropolis? Poets are notoriously liars or lovers, their hips made for hair pin turns at the public bar or the library counter — but dancing in the cemetery?

Imagine *Thriller* opium-slowed. The show begins in a field outside the cemetery — the first body moving above a verdigris-stained headstone — and I realise that what we're here to celebrate is the body, its dexterity and strength, its ability to do its own thing. Let it — inadvertent twitches in a dancer's face are a sign that living goes on. As I enter the cemetery a looped series of commands are played to the audience.

Depart with care
Walk with silence
Stay with your group
Do not look back

There's a blonde woman on a rope, above us, statue-still amongst the branches. She's wearing satin white underwear. As we pass underneath she moves into life, flexing the rope that we brush against as we pass. The orchestra at the base of the tree play as she twists, fish-lithe, to the song; then a male performer starts to ascend on another rope, legs angled in adductor locks, passing the female dancer who descends as he rises. I had walked past the male dancer a few moments before the show started, led by the funereal host's amber lantern, and he'd stood with his face in his hands as the audience were guided along the sodden path. The female dancer brings her performance to a halt with a sudden abrasive release of her body, her ankles now securely wrapped by the rope. Her body becomes rejected cargo, swinging from the tree.

There is now simultaneous movement behind numerous gravestones and in nettle-logged parts of the cemetery; the musical score holds them together through the patina of its ambient soundscape. Repetition and loop. A woman sits up high in a hula hoop; then a male dancer dances on a trampoline, also working a hoop, surrounded by the silent peninsula of the audience. He lets the hoop circle towards its final resting place on the trampoline and walks away towards the Scrapyard Meadow. The circle is the presiding symbol of the show. Eternal life. No beginning. No end.

Now all things rest
Darkness and light

I've spent whole days looking at stone mausolea — Thanatos and Hypnos poised over human remains — but have never been met with the possibility of human forms appearing from the earth, faces blanched, sinews flickering in the last of the summer light. Each body is orchestrated to be part of this bigger performance, but within that they are freeform; each body moves its own way — just once like this — within this moment.

There's an opera in the woods. A woman in blue, Eurydice, is dancing to the song of a woman dressed all in black. Before the song is finished, the audience is ushered forward by torch-bearing hosts, the hearse-people of the show. We walk past a projection of digital roses that animates a head stone, the last whorls of passing souls. The experience brings me closer to the strangers around me, shuffling stragglers walking a path through the mud. Some are shimmering in their glad rags, despite the Met Office's weather warning. Ankle cut jeans and hipster leather; look your best for the East End dead. There's a man with a ginger beard and Led Zeppelin T-shirt, a woman with grey hair wearing an oversized mac, a young couple giggling as they walk, then kissing under a rain-sodden sycamore. Sharing this death-changing experience, breathing in this festival of revenants. Living it.

I've always loved being alone in cemeteries, out of the crowd, the last person above ground, and I'm surprised to find that I'm not against sharing it with others. We *are* the audience. Bound as voyeurs. From the close attention that Tom's giving the technicalities of the show — photographing lighting systems and AV outputs — it won't be long until I find out.

A woman in the audience stands on an oak stump to get a better view. A man is performing above us, in Travolta whites, staring down with a purple determination flickering in his temples. I wonder what side the guides are on; with their amber torches attached to gnarly sticks, are they performers or audience?

They are somewhere in between, like a referee. Some are holding hands, thinking ahead to supper or last orders at the pub. A man in front of me is swinging his rucksack to the orchestra's lament. We're all *on the path* with everything in our lives still to play for. The rain's stopped. I get a closer view of Eurydice as she winds through the crowd; she's wearing blue dreadlocks. The cemetery has become an immersive theatre and we are all on this stage of real land and open air, connected through our movements, our energy.

As we walk along the track — through deep puddles and nettles fronding the brown soup of the mud — figures call us forward, with flames, towards abandoned paths. Cut sap hits the nostrils. A performer dances with the upside-down anchor of a crucifix held against his chest. Then the highpoint of the show happens. Two men are dancing together in white, supporting their bodies against the other. They hoist their bodies sideways like a flag — a static form counterbalanced against a wooden post. Then they somehow raise themselves up the poll in an entangled caul of limbs. One body levitates on the other. Sinks and rises. Strength in fusion.

This is live art as *memento mori*, a completely sensory experience. The two men descend the pole and walk away, breathing heavily, towards the high-rise flats that are blanched with mist.

No one seems to have noticed that it's started to rain. Water is dripping from the canopied roof of branches. We assemble in the open field that we started in — the man in the Led Zep T-shirt, the woman in the mac — to watch the final dance. A dance paced to the fugue of the pain of loss; the loss of love, that death known in life. The grief of Orpheus and Eurydice is played out in embraces, flourishes of dancers' bodies. Eurydice has made it this far through the winding paths of Tower Hamlets Cemetery Park, but not far enough to escape the loss that comes from a quick mistake. *Don't look back.* She breaks into a run, uplighters shadowing her body against the windblown trees. When the lights go out the crowd moves towards the cemetery entrance. Mile End Road welcomes us back to a familiar landscape, each of us more alert than when we entered two hours ago. Tom is frothing with ideas: we could put speakers behind graves, bring in an actor, a violinist, a nurse, a priest and a holy doctor. I'm ready to reconstruct my narrative of dead poets towards a live performance in the cemetery.

> Depart with care
> Walk with silence
> Stay with your group
> Do not look back

§

WILLIAM SPEAKS ————

There is another self that exists when sleeping in houses that are not our own. Ghosts come to us then. Eva, a spirit who was once a maid, is seven feet tall and only appears to women at the hinge of change. Last night I woke in the dark and stumbled to the bathroom, catching my foot on the plug of a phone charger — regaining my balance on the landing. A man I knew from daylight had arrived at the bathroom at the same time. I stared at him. Who was he? We looked at each other — I apologised — and we passed. In the morning the question wasn't 'who was he?' but 'who was I?' The private self was lost to the shuffling dreamer, exposed and inert, hidden behind the body's needs — with a quest to be lost in more sleep.

*To wake. To charge. To lose. To dream.*

# *The Charge*

## — HERBERT ERNEST HOWARD, SOLDIER POET

*As I came through the desert thus it was,*
*As I came through the desert: All was black,*
*In heaven no single star, on earth no track.*

B.V. THOMSON, *THE CITY OF DREADFUL NIGHT*

THE WAR MEMORIAL at the Southern Grove entrance is like a Modernist sculpture, an open-ended emporium listing the names of the dead from two wars. To read the names I need to step up and *in* to the memorial. Anyone listed over the age of 30 is ancient. And then come the names that seem to have disappeared from the English lexicon: Nettingham, Warcraft, Gilmerveen. Language dried, mushed and liquidated, bled into the loam. 'THEIR NAME LIVETH FOR EVERMORE.'

There's a poet recorded somewhere here: Herbert Ernest Howard. I scan in the half-light for his name. Howard died at Netley Hospital, Southampton on 24<sup>th</sup> July 1916. In the only remaining photograph he looks like a younger version of Siegfried

Sassoon; he has the same well-cut features, long nose, good skin. He left behind several poems which were later published in pamphlet form by his family. The cover states: 'SOLDIER POET... Wounded at Contalmaison. Died in course of an Operation at Netley Hospital... He was only 26 years of age.' The pamphlet is named *Verses from the Trenches: "The Charge" and Other Poems* and was published locally in Burcham Street, Poplar — just across Limehouse Cut.

I've brought Howard's pamphlet with me, downloaded to my phone. His poem 'A Call to You' can be read as a straightforwardly patriotic piece, beginning, 'Just pause, my lad, just pause, my lad; There's fighting to be done.' There are echoes here of the work of Jessie Pope, a female poet of the First World War who had never been to the front and whose poems were used as a tool to enthuse young men into signing up. I turn to Howard's next poem, 'The Charge', which seems to have been written after experiencing the trenches. Despite certain clunky elements (particularly in the metre and end-rhymes) the poem sears with invective descriptions.

> One night, 'twas like hell.
>   There were poisonous mists,
> Bombs, bullets, and shells —

My God! how they hissed.

The attack it was fierce:
   We were weary and worn.
They were trying to piece
   Our line a'fore dawn.

We laid in our trench.
   All sodden and soaked.
What with mud and the stench
   I thought we'd a'choked.

We would fire like the deuce.
   Then we'd cease a while.
The Huns — mad dogs loose —
   Lie there in a pile.

God! How the men swore —
   They all seemed possessed;
They were mad and, what's more,
   For nights they'd no rest.

There were parsons sons,
   Duke's sons, and others all mixed;
All handling their guns

And winning their tricks.

They were there for a purpose, and
    All of them meant
A fight to a close
    A'fore they'd relent...

Would we e'er see morn's gleam? —
    The thought never struck us;
We'd no time to dream.
    Only to fight and to "cuss".

The attack suddenly stopped:
    There was silence around.
The Huns, they'd hopped it;
    'Twas useless they found.

We raised one almighty shout —
    'Come, up lads and at 'em!'
Then our bayonets flashed out
    In the pale moonlight's gleam.

We leaped the trench, and on we went —
    Like devils we charged the mob;
For our mercy was spent and we

Felt and meant to make it a finished job.

We dashed into the crowd —
    My God! What a night;
How they yelled and they howled
    We thrust left and right.

We broke through their ranks;
    Then back we came.
On both of their flanks
    We played the same game.

We took their trench, mind, and
    If at your papers you'll glance,
They will describe just the kind
    Of the charges in France.

I look for Howard's name on the memorial wall, but it's nowhere to be seen. I might have more success by feeling along the raised text, reading it like braille. Two men walk through the entrance of the cemetery and as they become clearer through the gloom I see that one has a skinhead and the other a manbun. They contrast well, like Thomas Nashe's statement that the dove is for the day and the raven for the night. The two are deep in a conversation about the pending weekend, despite it only being Monday. Live for it. Mad for it. Paid for it, long before it's started. The cemetery is a place where the living form plans; a walk through the grounds adds a shot of serotonin to the planned *carpe diem*. A pair of joggers crunch past; one checks the face of his watch to ensure the 3,000th step doesn't go unacknowledged. Nothing gets in the way of the core. Grind the gravel to work the calves.

I look again at Howard's poem. Technically, the poem struggles through archaic expression and an overuse of the parlour room syntax of the previous century: 'The attack it was fierce.' This shadow of Victoriana is cut through with colloquialisms, some of which work okay, though they never give the reader the full sense of the language of the trenches which Isaac Rosenberg, for example, captured so well. The British Library website describes Howard's poems from *Verses from the Trenches* as 'patriotic in tone, describing the bravery of those who responded to the call to arms, about fighting for a just cause, and about his thoughts of home.' The ending of 'The Charge' can be read as confirming the stereotype of war, with the narrator stating that they captured the German trench — which is exactly what the reader will have heard in the newspapers. We know from the work of Sassoon and Wilfred Owen that these poets viewed their role as being to challenge the lies that were sold to the newspapers and 'to warn' readers of what war was like.

But there is perhaps another way to read Howard's poem. The colloquial tone of 'We would fire like the deuce' is more likely to be pastiche of an Officer than written in the poet's own voice. We know that Howard was a low-ranking soldier and would have identified more with 'the men' in the poem, rather than the orchestrating officer. It is here, I think, that we can take our hint to read the poem differently. Had Howard read the poems of Sassoon, particularly 'The General', and was he perhaps trying his hand at a sardonically-written dramatic monologue? When the narrator of the poem (as this seems to be) talks of how the men 'all seemed possessed', it is at this point we realise how he is talking of trench warfare as if it is sport. A closer look at the language shows a use of the following phrases to describe war: 'a game', 'a job', and 'winning... tricks'. It is this kind of mentality which *would* want the newspapers to confirm a high death toll of a nation's own army as a 'victory'.

Darkness has fallen in the cemetery now. The only light is from Howard's poem, illuminated on my screen. Voices distract me from the text. A man with an incredibly deep voice is agreeing with a woman in a denim jacket. I catch a single phrase on the breeze: "Yes, there's a lot of London in that."

I look again at the poem. Through this re-reading it is easy to see how the narrator's dismissal of the Germans as 'The Huns — mad dogs loose' and the British 'like devils... meant to make it a finished job' might not be Howard's view at all. This may have been a transitional poem in the development of Howard's poetry; he seems to be trying out something far more ambitious than in his poem 'A Call to You'. He is lacking the confident, satirical flourish of Sassoon, whose writing alerted the reader to the irony in the work, but with time Howard might have developed this.

I'm yet to find Howard's name on the memorial. The lights in the high-rise blocks on Southern Grove fade to maize yellow and from the balconies I can hear doors slamming, plates clattering and tempers fraying. Then laughter. Someone sings.

Then it's there, right in front of me: Howard's name and credentials: AGE 26, OXFORD & BUCKS LIGHT INFANTRY. 24.7.1916. I turn and look back into the cemetery. A silver wind spinner is turning one way, and then the next, in an uncertain wind. A bin top clatters. A pigeon comes soaring over the cemetery entrance as if to make it into the grounds before morning catches up with it. Then all birdsong is cancelled as a plane moves overhead — an evening flight from City Airport to Paris, Madrid, New York, Abu Dhabi. It passes and all is urban forest again.

I have a final walk to make, one that will take me deeper into the cemetery and into the night. Diane Kendall has detailed

Howard's actual grave for me and — with Howard's poem crystallising — I want to find his resting place. I head towards a part of the cemetery called Flander's Hollow; small crosses, like medals placed on long stems, stand along the path. One of them has been completely lifted from the ground by the swollen trunk of a tree; it hovers in abeyance as nature claims the territory. I shine my phone torch along the faces of the memorials; in the darkness it takes some time to find what I'm looking for — but there, semi-legible, with the text seeming to fade into the night, is Howard's resting place.

> In loving memory of our dear son Corp Herbert E. Howard
> who gave his life for his country 24th July 1916 age 26 yr
> "Now all that we can do is to morn for the dear one who was a
> soldier brave and true and has his duty done"
> also Pte Walter Howard of the Royal Fusiliers Brother of the above
> died 3rd Nov 1918 Labasse France age 32 yr. "Rest in Peace"

The Southern Grove gates are closed and I find my way along the footpath to the kissing gates on Hamlet's Way. As I approach the corner of Mile End Road I spot a bunch of wild pansies growing, almost inexplicably, near the curb.

Five paper ears — listening to the seeds speak.
Curling in the roar of night-time traffic.

§

WILLIAM SPEAKS ————

Someone I know lived in a Victorian house for years, then moved across the road to a house that was facing it. Why does this fascinate me? There is something of the doubling of the self in this; as if a life can be split and then watched at a distance. I stare at the old house from the window. The curtains move. Is it my reflection or is there someone inside? To see the space for what it is now — a house with a door, amidst dozens the same. The private space of the past seems accessible to the present self. And everything mirrored in reverse; the sun directly in the face, where it once warmed the back. If there is a way to trap time then perhaps this is it — to move to where the past can be viewed. The door knocks. A parcel is left.

*To light. To move. To open. To look.*

# Bad Onions

*But being there one feels a citizen;*
  *Escape seems hopeless to the heart forlorn:*
  *Can Death-in Life be brought to life again?*
  B.V. THOMSON, *THE CITY OF DREADFUL NIGHT*

THROUGHOUT THE 1880S AND '90s there were various attempts to
document the exact number of times Onions had been arrested,
but nobody seemed to know. Not even the police. Like black
mould, Onions was commonplace on the constabulary wall —
part of the East End brickwork — spreading his name from
one crime to the next, until he was known by everyone in east
London, then the whole of London, then nationally. He was viral
long before the internet, a meme before social media was even
dreamt of. Like Pete Doherty or Sid Vicious, every generation
needs an Onions; the press was so effusive that the journalists
almost became complicit in Onions' next crime. At last the Sugar
Maker was getting the audience he deserved.

In 1881 an Onions-related report appeared in *The
Nottingham Post*. Perhaps the local myth of Robin Hood captured
the reporter's imagination; here is Onions as the poor, intent on

dispensing justice to himself. Onions is depicted with white froth bubbling on his dehydrated tongue, fresh from an assault on a hairdresser — a symbol of all that was glamorous in the London that was alien to him (the typo in the name 'Onion' is true to the report).

> William Onion, 51, who was said to have been before the magistrates over 200 times, was charged at the Thames-street (London) Police Court yesterday with being drunk, disorderly and assaulting Inspector McCarthy, of the H-Division.
>
> About eight o'clock on Monday night the prisoner was taken to King David-lane station, Shadwell, charged with being drunk and disorderly, and committing an unprovoked assault on a hairdresser.
>
> At one o'clock Inspector McCarthy visited him in his cell, and noticed that the walls had been scandalously defaced. He spoke to the prisoner about it, on which Onion rushed at him and struck him a violent blow on the lip, cutting it; he then struck him in the face and, catching one of his fingers between his teeth, bit it severely.
>
> It took several men to overcome him and put the handcuffs on.
>
> Mr Saunders sentenced him to two months' hard labour, and said that if he came to the court again he would be sent to the sessions.

It is possible to read this episode as exposing Onions as a frustrated writer, one who had repressed his natural calling for so long that the words started to write themselves on the prison wall. A writer in the fire jacket of delirium tremens.

As is true to the definition of the poète maudit — the cursed poet living outside of society — Onions turned his invective against all symbols of authority. In August 1882 the *St. James Gazette* ran a report under the title 'A Frequent Offender'.

> At the Thames Police-court today, William Onion... was proved to have committed a violent and unprovoked assault on Police Constable David Griffiths, in Well-street, yesterday. It was stated that the prisoner had been before the magistrates over 200 times for various offences.
>
> Mr Saunders, in committing him to gaol for two months, with hard labour, said he was a disgrace to humanity, and expressed regret that he could not send him to penal servitude.

Well Street was part of an old country lane running from Shoreditch to Homerton, and was known for its market. Tesco was founded there by the 21-year-old Jack Cohen, who traded from a barrow among the many other stalls; rags to riches — with Onions flaunting the rags. Today, Onions would have had the security guard of any Tesco Express running in circles, with the self-checkout offering a free pass on its range of wines and liquors. Yet at this stage of his career as a petty criminal, theft was only a small aspect of his mission and the law itself was increasingly becoming the source of his acidity.

Five years passed until the next report. Onions is out of the city — on the north coast of Kent — and starving; he is reported as smashing the window of a shop in order to eat. On 12th November 1887, *The Whitstable Times and Hearne Bay Herald* reported the following:

> William Onion, 61, labourer was indicted at the Middlesex Sessions on Monday for maliciously damaging two plate-glass windows, value £7, the property of Mr. John Cairn, a licensed victualler.
>
> The prisoner, who said he had had nothing to eat for several days, deliberately broke two windows in the prosecutor's house and then gave himself up to the police.
>
> He now pleaded guilty, and 200 previous convictions were proved against him, some of them being for getting drunk, assaults, assaulting the police in the execution of their duty, robberies from the person, and one for manslaughter.

After commenting on such an extraordinary career, the Assistant-Judge passed upon the prisoner a sentence of 12 calendar months with hard labour.

This incident is no smash-and-grab from Onions; starved, he eats, then sits and waits for the police — placing himself back in the cycle of incarceration to which he had grown accustomed. It is, perhaps, due to these enforced breaks in drinking that he lived to such as old age.

On the 20th November 1888, *The Star* reported Onions as perpetrating violence against the police. In a reversal of power, it is Onions that follows the force back to their manor.

William Onion, the old man whom the Thames magistrate yesterday allowed to go free on a charge of drunkenness, went to the Shadwell Police-station last night and broke the window.

He told the magistrate this morning that policemen followed him about to lock him up for being drunk, and that he smashed the window to save himself from being locked up. (Laughter.)

Mr. Saunders said: "The Court stinks with your name, and you stand in such bad odour that all policemen look after you, knowing you are a dangerous man."

He would be sentenced to one month's hard labour.

All the signs are here of a man with nothing left to lose, courting his own downfall, turning his own descent into a paranoid game with The Peelers. Onions was caught in their dragnet, simultaneously resenting their oppression but inviting the fame that came from taking them on. It's worth bearing in mind that there were very good reasons why the working class of the East End hated the police. As Henry Mayhew documents in *London Labour and the London Poor*, even the costermongers — who had a much higher status than the destitute such as Onions — were vocal in their hatred for the police.

> 'Can you wonder at it, sir,' said a costermonger to me, 'that I hate
> the police? They drive us about, we must move on, we can't stand
> here, and we can't pitch there. But if we're cracked up, that is if we're
> forced to go into the Union (I've known it both at Clerkenwell and
> the City of London workhouses,) why the parish gives us money to
> buy a barrow, or a shallow, or to hire them, and leave the house and
> start for ourselves: and what's the use of that, if the police won't let us
> sell our goods?—Which is right, the parish or the police?'

A more specific gripe for Noctavigants such as Onions was the role the police played in making sure the poor got no sleep on London's streets. To the police the bodies of the poor were an acrid and endless drip through the night's calcified funnel. Can you imagine being deprived all day of food and warmth, without any semblance of anything merry or enlivening; and just as sleep finds you in some doorway or alley — to put a temporary cloak over reality — a policeman shines a torch in your face and tells you to move on? Jack London learned this first-hand.

> It was this sleeping that puzzled me. Why were nine out of ten of them asleep or trying to sleep? But it was not till afterwards that I learned. It is a law of the powers that be that the homeless shall not sleep by night. On the pavement, by the portico of Christ's Church, where the stone pillars rise toward the sky in a stately row, were whole rows of men lying asleep or drowsing, and all too deep sunk in torpor to rouse or be made curious by our intrusion.

The poor were viewed as a collective vermin, sprawling through the city at night — a blackened spillage collapsing on London's green spaces.

There is a Dickensian surrealism to *The Illustrated Police News* report on 25th January 1896 which documents the strange dialogue which took place between Onions and the fittingly named Mr Mead.

> William Onions, otherwise known as "Spring Onions" — sixty-two, who has been convicted of drunkenness some hundreds of times,

was again charged with a similar offence.

Onions said he had nothing to say to the charge, but wished to make a statement about another matter that had been weighing on his mind.

Last September he went to Selby in Yorkshire, and was an inmate of the infirmary in that town for five weeks. After his recovery he was made wardsman, and had to assist a nurse. The latter said to him one day, 'Do you think it wrong to relieve persons who are suffering from incurable pain?'

At the time he did not think much of the remark, but during the short time he was there no fewer than seven deaths occurred. There was a man suffering from a terrible cancer in the cheek, and one morning the nurse said to him (Onions), 'Put this pill in his mouth'. Without thinking, he did so, and the man died four or five hours after.

The matter had been on his conscience ever since, and on Monday he was going to the police, but got drunk.

Onions appealed for leniency.

Mr. Mead: No one has had more indulgence and consideration, and this is the way you show your gratitude. Like a criminal fool that you are, you go and indulge in drink when you know you should not touch it. You will go to prison for one month with hard labour. When in prison you can write to the Local Government Board with reference to the statement.

What is documented here is Onion's role in euthanasia. Under the directive of a nurse who was committed to ending the lives of those in incurable pain, Onions administers a pill to a man who dies, as a result, a few hours later. This insight into Onions's psyche is revealing on a number of levels. First of all, it is significant that this breakthrough to his conscience came through not being *told* to do something — as he'd spent his whole life experiencing — but through being asked a question by the nurse: 'Do you think it wrong to relieve persons who are suffering from incurable pain?' There was clearly something in this moral prompt which acted as an inner jolt, rousing Onions to think about his relationship with the people around him. This seems to have triggered an ethical response in him, leading him to question the role he had played — and could play — for both good and evil. The fact he was then told by the nurse to give a pill to a dying man — whose cheek was eaten by cancer — seems to have both enlivened and frightened him. Did he, perhaps, question his role as a murderer in this incident? And if so, did this then push back on to his other crimes, manslaughter included, acting as the stirring of conscience that led to a moral awakening?

The police records for 1898 show Onions in a particularly bad state. Following various convictions, the Sugar Maker had given his occupation on different occasions as 'stevedore', 'composer' and — in a glimpse of the life that was about to open for him — 'versifier'. On this occasion he was described as having a broken nose, but being able to read and write. By December of that year he had moved to Doncaster where he was convicted for damaging a window. The end of the year saw him arrested in Pontefract for further drink-related misdemeanours.

Nobody, least of all Onions, would have expected that his own salvation would come from the most unlikely of sources, one that can run through a person like a hidden vein and has been known to govern the direction of a life with a force stronger than fate.

Poetry.

§

WILLIAM SPEAKS ──────

I'm trying to describe my dream to someone but the fierce light of the past days has changed to a leaden grey. The winds are uprooting the softened roots of the marigolds. "We were in our old house," I tell her, "and the house was haunted." At that moment I remember the root meaning of 'haunt', which is to 'frequent' — to habitually visit a place. "We lived there for 35 years," I tell her. I remember how each room we walked towards had a kind of invisible hand pulling us into it — at least that's how it felt. A secret force that was as reassuring as it was terrifying. On the landing, my son began to rise up to the ceiling but I grabbed his feet. "Say The Lord is My Shepherd," he shouted, and I did.

Outside the window, leaves fawn the glass, soon to be debris. "Then I received a text on my phone," I tell this person. "It said: look out of the window." I pulled back the curtains in disbelief: the garden was animated with summer. Then I saw my mother laying down, sunbathing, as she used to do for whole days at a time, 30 years ago. I forgot to ask her, in the dream, who had sent the text — was it her, or the ghost?

*To dream. To hold. To place. To tell.*

# *Two of the Williams*
## — IVATTS AND SHERRARD

*The nudity of flesh will blush though tameless,*
*The extreme nudity of bone grins shameless,*
*The unsexed skeleton mocks shroud and pall.*
B.V. THOMSON, *THE CITY OF DREADFUL NIGHT*

IN THE 21ST CENTURY does a poet need to write a poem to qualify as a poet? Following the invention of the 'One-Word Poem' by Ian Hamilton Finlay in the late 1960s, the lid on the gunpowder has been loose. A new generation have used viruses and algorithms to distort texts, creating images that are then presented as the finished poetic work — with or without surface text. Poetry has become a way of thinking, a space in which concepts are invented and presented to others, a static energy that can only be detected in a certain breeze. Words are optional.

This is useful for me to remember as the two poets I'm looking for — Willian Ivatts and William Sherrard — might not be poets at all; but then there's always the chance that I could present whatever I find on their headstones as the work itself.

Their names have been given to me by Diane Kendall. I want to scour every inch of ground in the hope of claiming them. The search might become a conceptual poem in itself: *Invisible Pastoral for Two Williams*. I'll need my torch; the last of the sun is sliding like butter down the glass of a nearby high-rise.

I shine my phone on a headstone and see a trellis of ivy like a crack; its leaves are spreading crabwise for purchase on the surface. A man walks past me in a bright yellow workman's vest, the purple shield of the West Ham badge pressed into the back. His Staffordshire Bull Terrier sniffs my shoes, then follows after the golden hammers.

I follow my map — a crumpled flannel under torchlight — to an intersection of paths; it's amongst these headstones that I find Ivatts.

A LIFE DEVOTED TO ARCHAEOLOGY, LITERATURE AND
ART.
Died at S. Hackney 3rd Feb 1911. Aged 92.

Close to two centuries of learning are buried in the ground beneath my feet. Fought-for knowledge, long before the days of upload and share. Ivatts' world would have been formed from boxes filled with cantos and quartos, shelves of foxed books.

There is no evidence here that Ivatts wrote poetry, although the grief he must have experienced would have added pigment to his tapestry. His headstone also lists his daughters Ellen, who died in 1861 at just 14 months, Alice, who died in 1871 at 22, and Emma, who died in 1878 aged 24 years. Ivatts is also buried with his wife, Martha. The stone is corroded near the base. Perhaps there was a poem here, before time weathered it to nothing?

I've followed Ivatts as far as a I can. The British Library, the National Poetry Library, the omphalos of Google — none of them yields clues to him being a poet. I shine my torch across his grave for the final time and a moth moves from behind the stone; it's a bucks butterfly — yellow origami — searching for the females who are yet to emerge.

I've drifted off towards the Thames-side of the cemetery; the kissing gates on Ackroyd Drive make a rusty, swine-like hiss as someone leaves the grounds. Whenever it gets dark here I make the mistake of thinking I'm the last person alive. But living bodies are everywhere — commuting, talking, waiting. I remember that line from *Anthony and Cleopatra*: 'Thou hast seen these signs — / They are black vesper's pageants'. The pageantry runs all night here and I'm starting to read the signs.

As I'm checking my map for William Sherrard's headstone

something bites into my calf. My body jolts forward and I look back, expecting a snake, and see a lolling nettle. As I continue walking, the darkness escalates the sting into a war scar, the tiny smart amplifying into an imagined catastrophe. This is the kind of magnification of experience that Thomas Nashe is referring to when he talks of the night transforming the mind: 'And as the firmament is still moving and working, so uncessant is the wheeling and rolling on of our brains, which every hour are tempering some new piece of prodigy or other, and turmoiling, mixing and changing the course of our thoughts'. I grip a tree stump and tell myself to leave the psychodrama to dead poets.

A train passes across Cantrell Road, clattering heavily on the wet rails. Then, almost inexplicably, birdsong. A dusk chorus harmonises in the gloaming. I realise I'm following the outskirts of the cemetery and see something yellow on the wall: the name *Ana* written as graffiti. The wind blusters up into the trees which tower, tyrant-like, over the low cemetery wall. It would only take a short bunk up for the Resurrectionists to make it in here — but why would they bother? The gates are always open.

I've reached the urban forest past midnight. There's a density to the overgrowth here, a flush of green signalling unbridled nature. Cow parsley lolls like the heads of sleeping Quakers and the sycamores make a run for the moon. There are no graves —

and where there are no graves there is every chance of forgotten poets. The common ground is a wild, unreadable sanctuary. As Catherine Arnold explains in *Necropolis*, the majority of the many burials in the 19th century were in pauper graves, paid for at 25s each: 'with excellent financial returns derived from a policy of filling common graves as full as possible and packing them together as densely as possible'. What sounds like a new method of packing consumables was a sales pitch aimed at those who would know good economic sense when they heard it. Even if the buyers knew they were in the supply category of this financial ecosystem. By 1850, 80 percent of burials here were of paupers.

Broken graves make found poems. I shine my torch and one appears as if bitten, a crescent moon wiped out from the side. The remaining texts swims in formless syntax:

*ALS*
  *HUSBAND*
*WHO DEPAR*

*OCT BER 18 1*

*ROCK OF A*
*LET ME HIDE*

A text primed for social media. Photo and post for Instafame. 'Rock of a / Let me hide' captures the warring introvert and extrovert that characterises so many poets — the solid exterior shielding the urge to shrink like a mollusc from the world's boot. I follow along Southern Grove, past dog walkers leading a party of psychotic greyhounds. A terrier called Ruby is frothing-up with an orange ball in its mouth. "You lost ya ear 'oles?" the owner shouts.

It's hard to describe what it feels like to find a poet's grave in the dark of night – it lies somewhere between a dream and deja-vu, like bumping into the person who waved you off at the airport thousands of miles away. London stops momentarily and pays homage to poetry, then speeds off again, accelerating towards the Blackwall Tunnel.

Above the Celtic rose cut into the stone: THE FAMILY GRAVE OF WILLIAM SHERRARD. His wife's name is above his: SARAH ELEANOR GERRARD. DIED AGED 60 YEARS. This is the lushest part of the cemetery, at the nexus of the Poplar Wood, Ash Wood and High Glade. A fox trots out from a fused hedge of nettle and cow parsley, its eyes lava-lit in the dark, and crosses the path to the other side. I stand with Sherrard for a while.

William Sherrard is my first discovery of his kind: a poet only evidenced by the poem that occupies their headstone. This is a cunning move, side-stepping the bruising net-and-ball process of publication and review. His work is not only available a hundred years after his death, but the content of the poem makes strong claims for the merits of his work, and his qualities as a man.

The Bromley poet has gone to rest
Of all the men he was one of the best
He was honest, just and kind
Many more like him are left behind

Sherrard's address is listed as Botolph Road, Bromley. Botolph is the saint who gave his name to the literary journal published in Cambridge in 1956 which first included the work of Ted Hughes. It was at the launch party of the *St Botolph's Review* that Hughes met Sylvia Plath and she bit his cheek until it bled. I wonder if Botolph is a brighter omen for the poetic path laid out by Sherrard? Botolph: patron saint of wayfarers. The churches at the entrances to the four gates of the City were named after him. There is more known about Botolph than Sherrard. Neither the libraries nor the databases have any poetry by him, suggesting his work never made it to print — not even in the student review.

Rain bristles through trees. A creature scratches at the earth. Looking through the document given to me by Diane

Kendall, I suspect that Sherrard wrote the poem for his headstone himself. I then see that in addition to this poem there is also one for his wife, who died six weeks before her husband. Sherrard, as The Bromley Poet, was quick with his pen and there is a clear similarity in style with the poem above:

A light is from our household gone
All we love is stilled
A place is vacant in our home
Which never can be filled.

Poetry has placed a stake in the ground here; if Sherrard had space and more time he might have written enough to fill the tower of St Botolph without Aldgate. Maybe he did and it remained in a trunk after his death? The grave here has the hallmark of being Sherrard's plan, executed by a Victorian momentarily in control of one aspect of his ailing life — the tailoring of the headstone. This stone, that contains some of Sherrard's last thoughts, is being eaten away by time, limescale and what seems to be rust from the internal support. I suspect Sherrard wrote this when he was 'on his lasties', as we say in Liverpool. The towering trees seems to hood me in with Sherrard, under the darkness, as the leaves delay the drip of the rain long after it's landed above us. I smell cigarette smoke; someone else is around, out of sight.

When Sherrard's son, John Silk, died in 1926, the remaining space on the headstone was given to a final couplet, this time from a truncated line from The Gospel According to Matthew.

> Come unto me all that are weary
> And I will give you rest.

'Well have the poets termed the night the nurse of cares', Nashe wrote, 'the mother of despair'. How late is it? It's nearly two in the morning. It's a bed I want now, not the rest of the grave. I've been here long enough to know the difference.

§

WILLIAM SPEAKS ———

I'm moving away by train again, at 7.20 in the morning. At Runcorn the sun rises like a pink albumen, is shredded by the crosshatch of a bridge. Pink bleeds yellow, then bleeds orange. I think of Mallarmé's poems for Anatole, his son. Anatole was Mallarmé's second son and had contracted rheumatic fever, dying of an enlarged heart in 1879, aged eight. Mallarmé tried to write a four-part tombeau — a composition for the dead. This form, the tomb poem, had the aim of capturing grief in the objective concretism of verse. The boy's enlarged heart, the father's over-thinking. Mallarmé scratched at page after unyielding page, pressed ink-clot into ink, hoping it would collapse into form. It never did. 212 pages of fragmentary notes, each jagged with the condensed salt of the unbearable. The compaction wouldn't yield to acceptance. After Mallarmé's death, Modernism moved the work forward with grief's broken hindwing. Put the poems away now, the work is done.

*To rise. To bleed. To write. To work.*

# A Whitechapel Day of the Dead

*The City rests for man so weird and awful,*
*That his intrusion there might seem unlawful,*
*And phantoms there may have their proper home.*

B.V. THOMSON, *THE CITY OF DREADFUL NIGHT*

THE GHOST OF ISAAC ROSENBERG, sunken-eyed and trench-coated, lurks around the Whitechapel Gallery. I'm here to talk about my journeys into the Magnificent Seven with the artists French and Mottershead. I imagine Rosenberg as a vapour in a black mac, circling the centre of his creative world. Rosenberg provides a sardonic sneer to poetry as a tub-thumping platform for patriotism. It was here in 1914 that he exhibited his paintings. A few years before he'd self-published a pamphlet of poems, *Night and Day*. Rosenberg's rain-soaked brooding is the antithesis of Rupert Brooke's perky optimism. Rosenberg's 'On Receiving News of the War' is one of the few poems to document the news of 1914 with despair. In a visionary flourish he calls forth what would be the prevailing image of the war — crimson red blood, feeding the poppies:

O! ancient crimson curse!
Corride, consume.
Give back this universe
Its pristine bloom.

I'm at the Gallery this evening, just two miles from Tower Hamlets Cemetery Park, to take part in a Day of the Dead event. Cultural magus and poet Gareth Evans is hosting proceedings. Whip-slim from swift and effortless hurdling from one artform to another, Evans's email footers contain more culture than the quarterly bulletin at the ICA. As well as curating moving image at the Whitechapel Gallery, he's a regular at the National Poetry Library, slipping in and out of the book stacks with intent to surface forgotten poets. He was the first to put me onto American hermit poet Alfred Starr Hamilton. Evans is used to working with the biggest names in visual art, but he's also an exploder of binaries and knows that the cultural map is just as likely to shift through the excavation of a discontinued lyric as it is from staging the latest immersive installation.

Halloween sits highest amongst my annual cycle of rituals; a gateway to the year's end — that feeling of frequenting familiar territory. As a child my mum would carve out a turnip. The Hollywood-glow of the pumpkin was yet to hit Liverpool. My younger brother and I would carry them into the streets, swinging on strings. Their yellow-green faces like minks with cirrhosis. Now I take the day off work and savour every moment of the declining light. I loved the 10 years of taking my son out for Trick or Treating, followed by duck-apple and a shared reading of Poe's 'The Raven'. If there are moments of the year which somehow emanate through the people we are, then this is mine. If we can choose to return as ghosts when we're dead, I'll be living for the cliché of coming back to haunt on Halloween.

Gareth kicks off the event in a way that makes his own technician jolt. He strides on stage wearing a silver skull. Tom Lehrer's 'We Will All Go Together When We Go' provides the soundtrack for this piece of extempore theatre. When the song ends, Evans speaks through the narrow slit in the mask; the microphone spits as the words squeeze out. Eloquent as the Reaper's silence, Evans outlines his own vision of the dead:

A lot of events have corpsed or died in this room, hopefully this one won't, other than in the way it's meant to. We're here to celebrate the one place we all meet, despite our different views on Brexit. Today is the Mexican Day of the Dead, which is why we're delighted to gather here together quite a few thousand miles from that particular death cult, to celebrate death, to think about it out loud, to share ideas on death, to look at how death has been portrayed in various aspects of culture. To engage head-on with it, both past, present and probably future — given that all of us will share that wonderful encounter at some point. Hopefully reasonably smoothly and easily, without too much pain, but wherever we go we're going together, although we go privately, of course, when we do actually go … Which is what our various performers will be focused on, including of course the great Victorian cemeteries which have circled our Metropolis and which include the famous dead and the not-so famous dead. Those dead are absolutely crying out through the six feet of topsoil to be heard, to be found again and to be renamed, rediscovered and re-lauded, and that's exactly what the poet, cultural activist, librarian and all-round performance person Chris McCabe will be doing very shortly when he takes us on his tour through London's cemeteries...

I smart in my seat, thinking of the Tower Hamlets dead and the responsibility I've given myself to document them — to make sure these voices are heard loud and clear, or at least with the genuine scuff of Electronic Voice Phenomena. I take the microphone and open with the W.B. Yeats' quote: 'the living can assist the imagination of the dead'. I then turn to Malcolm Lowry's *Under the Volcano*. I read a section in which the sozzled Geoffrey Firmin falls to the floor in a cantina, banging his body on a ledge on the way down. Then I line up my dead poets, as if bringing them on stage, and introduce them like family. I end with the showman in the pack: William 'Spring' Onions.

I take my seat, unprepared for what French and Mottershead present. They take to the stage to introduce the work then quickly leave; the live static of the microphone seems to be sucked into a vacuum, the hiss replaced with pure silence. On the screen there are moving images of an urban woodland, which could easily be a section of Tower Hamlets Cemetery Park. Then a woman's voice can be heard through the speakers — with the timbre of a voice actor pitching yoghurt — transmitting the artists' words into the space. We're being treated to a lovingly forensic treatment of what exactly happens to the body after death. The experience stays in my memory long after the event:

THE WARM EARLY EVENING SUMMER SUN FILTERS THROUGH THE LEAVES OF THE OAK AND BEECH TREES AND FALLS ACROSS YOUR BODY ... YOU'RE ON YOUR BACK, ARMS BY YOUR SIDES, YOUR EYES AND MOUTH ARE OPEN ... YOUR MUSCLES RELAX AND YOUR BODY EASES INTO THE GRASS BENEATH YOU ... BLOOD DRAINS FROM YOUR FACE ... IT SINKS TO THE BACK OF YOUR BODY ... YOUR COOLING BODY HEAT IS BEING TAKE AWAY ON THE BREEZE AND DRAWN DOWN INTO THE GROUND ... YOUR LIPS DRY OUT ...

THE MUSCLES CONTROLLING YOUR STOMACH AND INTESTINES SLACKEN ... YOUR SPHINCTER'S OPEN AND THE CONTENTS OF YOUR BOWEL AND BLADDER LEAK OUT .... CELLS USE UP THE REMAINING OXYGEN IN YOUR BLOOD AND BODY ... ATTRACTED BY THE FEINT FIRST ODOURS OF YOUR DECOMPOSING TISSUES A FLY LANDS ON YOUR CHEEK AND EXPLORES YOUR FACE ... IT'S LOOKING FOR A WARM AND MOIST OPENING ... IT TAKES A FEW STEPS OVER YOUR BOTTOM LIP AND INTO YOUR MOUTH ... LAYS OVER 300 EGGS AND LEAVES ... FLIES CONTINUE TO ARRIVE ... AS THE PATCH OF EVENING SUNLIGHT MOVES OVER YOUR BODY THE AIR COOLS ... YOU'RE STILL COOLING ... YOUR FACE AND NECK TIGHTEN ... YOUR JAW LOCKS ... DAY BREAKS AND RISING ACID CONGEALS YOUR BLOOD ... YOU'RE STILL COOLING ... THE FAT IN YOUR SKIN SOLIDIFIES ... BACTERIA INVADES YOUR VEINS ... COLOURING THEIR INTERCLOCKING PATCHES DEEP PURPLE AND GREEN ... THE PATCH OF WARM SUNLIGHT PASSES OVER YOUR BODY ... YOU'RE NO LONGER COOLING ... YOU'VE REACHED THE TEMPERATURE OF THE WOODLAND AROUND YOU .... YOUR JAW SLACKENS ... YOUR MUSCLES AND ORGANS SOFTEN ... YOUR SMELL INTENSIFIES AS THE DAY WARMS .... YOUR TISSUES ARE SOFT AND DOUGHY ... THE FIRST BATCH OF BLOWFLY

EGGS HATCH ... YOUR COAGULATED BLOOD BECOMES LIQUID AGAIN ... THE OUTERSMOST LAYER OF YOUR SKIN SLIPS AND SEPARATES FROM THE LAYER BELOW ... VAPOURS LEAK FROM EVERY ORIFICE ... YOUR TONGUE SWELLS OUT OF YOUR MOUTH .... YOUR ABDOMEN BECOMES MASSIVELY DISTENTED ... UNDER PRESSURE THE GASES BLOW YOU UP ... BUTTONS POP ... SEAMS AND FABRIC RIP ... LARGE MASSES OF MAGGOTS WORM THROUGH YOUR HEAD DEVOURING YOUR BRAINS ... THE COLONY IS WORKING DEEPER INTO YOUR BRAIN ... YOU ARE GETTING WARMER ... DECOMPENSATION FLUIDS FLOOD OUT OF YOUR BODY ... POISONING THE GROUND ... SAPLINGS AND SHOTS WILT AND WITHER ... SOME OF THE USUAL ANIMALS ARE FORCED AWAY ... YOU'RE THE CENTRE OF A SCORCHED ISLAND ...

I'm thinking of the bodies of the Williams. I am used to thinking of dead poets as living on in their work, but have never considered them as having lived on in the ground — investing the soil with a richness that has added to London's wild spaces. As the soundscape turns to a description of the body in autumn, it's William 'Spring' Onions who comes to mind now.

IT'S AUTUMN ... YOU'RE COVERED BY A DECOMPOSING

BLANKET OF LEAVES ... BY SPRING YOUR LEAF COVER
HAS FALLEN THROUGH YOUR SKELETON ... BLUEBELLS
FERTILISED BY YOUR NUTRIENTS SURROUND YOUR
ISLAND ... HIGH ABOVE YOU SOME OF YOUR NUTRIENTS
HAVE ALREADY MADE THEIR WAY UP THE LEAVES OF
THE OAK AND BEECH TREES ... YOU'RE SETTLING INTO
THE SOIL AND THE SEASONAL CYCLE ... BY EACH SPRING
A LITTLE LESS OF YOU IS VISIBLE ... ROOTS ENTER IN
YOUR TEETH AND SKULL ... THE DECADES MOVE ON
AND YOU GO DEEPER ... THE STRUCTURE OF YOUR
SKELETON UNDERGOES A GENTLE COLLAPSE ... THESE
DEPOSITS ARE THE INITIAL STAGES OF FOSSILISATION
... YOUR BONES BECOME STONE

Death is a great editor. There are more stages to the post-death
body than the wake, the burial, the zombie and the skeleton. In
essence the dead body is living. Perhaps we should take a lead from
the cultures that count the age of a person from their conception,
and define a person's final age as the moment nature stops living
on their body? The body is an island that continues to drift and
brings so many urgent species to its shores.

After the event the books are cleared from the signing
table and a man in his 60s lies down on it, crossing his arms
across his chest. A crowd gathers around and takes photographs,
before the security guard ushers us towards the doors. I make for

the steps of Aldgate East station, on the lookout for the ghost of Rosenberg, but it's another dead poet that comes to me now, the French Surrealist Robert Desnos. His poem 'Le Cimetiere' is propelled by a vision of the poet's own dead body after death in which the earth grows rich on his nutrients.

> Under these three trees, nowhere else, is my burial-place.
> I pluck from them spring's first and earliest leaves
> Between a marble column and a granite base.
> [...]
> With an ink more liquid than blood and the water of fountains
> Can I protect my memory from forgetting
> As a cuttlefish spends its blood and breath, retreating?
>
> Can I protect my memory from forgetting?
>
> *(translated by Timothy Adès)*

The Tube arrives and I board, but my mind is two miles back, in the cemetery, thinking of the dead bodies of the poets. Can I protect the memory of their poems from forgetting?

§

Frederick Fleet, the lookout on the *Titanic*, was abandoned by his father and never knew his mother. He was given to a Barnardo's home, then handed on to a seaman's orphanage. When I take my son fishing, or out on his bike — or to play football — the Gothic gables of the orphanage rise over the park. Once I tried to book tickets for a night-time séance but I received a message saying Health and Safety wouldn't agree to it. I have, however, walked inside the building. After the orphanage was closed in the 1940s it was turned into a mental hospital. As I walked through the building, I was surrounded by beds, wheelchairs, crutches. A three-piece band were playing live. Stalls had been set-up in the old orphanage canteen; a woman was selling biscuits, a man showing photographs of birds. Did this really take place? When Fleet saw the iceberg he rang the bell three times and phoned the bridge. His job was done. Later, he said he would have seen the iceberg sooner if he'd been given binoculars, but this was not standard practice on White Star Line ships. The history of the century stuck to him like dog hair. For the rest of his life the crew on other ships considered him bad luck. He worked in a ship repair yard, then sold newspapers on Pound Tree Road, Southampton. A week after his wife died, Fleet hung himself in the garden of his brother-in-law's house. This was 1963; the Beatles were number one in the charts. On the centenary of the sinking of the *Titanic* someone left binoculars on Fleet's grave, with a note: 'Fred, you could have done with these'.

*To remain. To see. To hang. To sink.*

# A Pea-souper at the Aldgate Pump

## — WILLIAM J. PEARSON

*The massy iron gates were both withdrawn;*
*And every window of its front shed light,*
*Portentous in that City of the Night.*

B.V. THOMSON, *THE CITY OF DREADFUL NIGHT*

FINDING WILLIAM J. PEARSON (1832-92) isn't as easy as my map makes out. With dead poets it never is; in the twilight, songwriters can be just as elusive. Out on Hamlets Way a woman is shouting to a man, "it's by that tree... no, that tree there!" Are they looking for Pearson too? They're pointing the wrong way; their mission is outside the cemetery, the dark island I've marooned myself on.

At night Google Maps morphs my movements into a blue dot, an orb of data that gives me a compass direction in relation to the vast ocean of London, *out there*, beyond the gates. But its detailed mapping ends within the walls itself; none of the named sections — and certainly none of the monuments — are shown on my screen. Have I moved into Lodge Wood, or am I still in

Sanctuary Wood? Google moves my blue dot like a blowfish in an aquarium. I'm heading north towards Pearson.

As I walk under an empire of trees, I think of how the woodlands are known as 'multi-storeyed', and how that echoes the many high-rise apartments of the East End. Above me are limber sycamores, cancelling out the ever-present urban light. Then there is a whole layer of wildflowers, ferns, mosses and deadwood occupying the ground. Beneath me are the dead bulbs of previous decades. The sound of a man scraping his feet startles me, then a dog smarts on a lead as they pass me with purpose. Work. Dinner. Walk. Bed.

As with many of the Magnificent Seven poets, I've found Pearson wasn't born in London but was summoned here, as if by a calling. In 1874 William Booth, the founder and first general of the Salvation Army, sent Pearson a letter asking him to come to London and join The Christian Mission. Pearson responded positively, 'fell in love' with Booth and became Superintendent of the Shoreditch Circuit. Pearson was in a position to allow his radiant love of Christ to cut through the East End fog. I walk past a two-tone fox, ripped to the ribs. It stops and looks back at me like the creature from Von Trier's *Antichrist*. I expect it to offer me crack. Then it slips away, leaving a bunch of leaves lolling on a branch.

Pearson became the Manager of the Book Stores for the Salvation Army. Cyril Barnes described him as taking a 'sleeves rolled up' approach to his work. Pearson led on the Salvation Army publication *The War Cry* and it became the platform for many of his songs and poems. On one occasion an issue was printed in a run of 17,000 copies and Pearson had to stand guard over it as a dense pea-souper descended on London.

> When the fog was at its worst and hopes were lowest, an anonymous member of the staff groped his way along the streets in search of a cab. At last, by Aldgate Pump, he found a solitary vehicle whose owner had given up hope of reaching home and had decided to make the best of what shelter his cab could afford.

Pearson was born in Derby into a Primitive Methodist family. There is an account of him, as a boy, being stolen by a sailor and narrowly being saved by his father before being taken away to sea. There is something of Huckleberry Finn in the young Pearson, who always seemed to be pushing out for new territory. 'School had little attraction for a lad,' Barnes writes, '[he was] more interested in the purpose and working of the stars and sun, and often the surrounding woods and the company of questionable companions were preferred to the classroom.' Before he changed his lifestyle he was known for smoking, drinking, attending music halls and 'smashing gates and locks during night escapades'. Like Onions, he was a creature of the night; poetry found its place in the mythology of both men's recovery. As Pearson would later write:

> … God changed my heart,
> With bad companions I did part;
> For mercy I did loud implore,
> When kneeling on a cold brick floor;
> Soon pardon came, my load was gone.

Once he had taken up his position within the Salvation Army, Pearson's devotion to God bordered on the maniacal. He would pin the names of those he wanted to see converted on a box. Pearson gave up on sleep to read the Bible. On one occasion he fell asleep in a fire-grate.

It's too dark to see now so I stick to the path, following the Lime Tree Walk to the Round Glade. A couple stop me and ask if there's an exit anywhere. I point them to the one halfway down Hamlets Way. Everyone wants out — I want Pearson. The rain starts to fall heavily. In the silty half-light, all of the converted flats look like monster doss-houses. Branches are flung across the paths like shipwrecks. The headstones have given up their identities and present themselves in a uniform shroud. The night protects its interns.

In his first year at the Salvation Army, Pearson had connected 400 people with God. His main meeting room was the Apollo Music Hall on Hare Street. 'This building,' Barnes writes, 'loaned by a firm of brewers, and which had echoed to the sound of comic songs and ribald laughter and been filled with the smell of smoke and beer during the week, on Sundays became the spiritual birthplace of many an East-End sinner.' Pearson would poach human souls from the bird markets on Sclater Street and Hare Street. People congregated there on Sundays to buy caged chaffinches, goldfinches, starlings and thrushes, and it proved good hunting grounds for Pearson. I shine my torch along the headstones. The grave of William James Smellie, and the Smellie family, are buried beneath the most pristine and well-kept granite memorial I've seen today.

Most of Pearson's work was in trying to steer the drunken classes of Bethnal Green and Stoke Newington onto the right path of God — a little like fighting a forest fire with an apothecary jar of Holy Water. At open air meetings, groups of drinkers would gather and cajole the missionaries with their casks of ales. On one occasion Pearson improvised a poem on the spot.

Once again I charge you stop,
  For unless you warning take,
Ere you are aware you'll drop
  Into the burning lake.

The popularity of Pearson's approach swelled when the Salvation Army set up the People's Mission Hall in Whitechapel. The Hall offered cheap tea and coffee, soup and Australian sheep's tongues for a penny. The way to the souls of the poor is through sustenance — it's hard to believe in an afterlife on an empty stomach.

Jack London writes less positively about his experience of the Salvation Army in *The People of the Abyss*. Following a night of 'carrying the banner', he walks south through the early hours of the morning in the hope of a free breakfast.

It was a weary walk. Down St. James Street I dragged my tired legs, along Pall Mall, past Trafalgar Square, to the Strand. I crossed the Waterloo Bridge to the Surrey side, cut across to Blackfriars Road, coming out near the Surrey Theatre, and arrived at the Salvation Army barracks before seven o'clock. This was "the peg" and by "the peg," in the argot, is meant the place where a free meal may be obtained … Now, about the Salvation Army in general I know nothing, and whatever criticism I shall make here is of that particular portion of the Salvation Army which does business on Blackfriars

Road near the Surrey Theatre. In the first place, this forcing of men who have been up all night to stand on their feet for hours longer, is as cruel as it is needless. We were weak, famished, and exhausted from our night's hardship and lack of sleep, and yet there we stood, and stood, and stood, without rhyme or reason.

I've arrived where Pearson should be: Square 36, located along the Holly Walk. Through the dark I see a stone broken into an assemblage of pieces, a portmanteau of parts disowning their provenance. I push back the grass and find a single piece of text: A.R. ADAMS. POPLAR. Not the names of the buried this time, but the maker of the stone.

In 1878 Pearson was sent to extend his mission in the notorious Ancoats area of Manchester. 35 years before, Friedrich Engels had spent a number of years around Ancoats writing *The Conditions of the Working Class in England*.

Everywhere half or wholly ruined buildings, some of them actually uninhabited, which means a great deal here; rarely a wooden or stone floor to be seen in the houses, almost uniformly broken, ill-fitting windows and doors, and a state of filth! Everywhere heaps of debris, refuse, and offal; standing pools for gutters, and a stench which alone would make it impossible for a human being in any degree civilised to live in such a district.

Pearson was given the use of a music hall. His audiences grew to up to 900 people, which annoyed the owner of the Hall who had never seen such a big audience in his venue, but an audience unwilling to queue for the beer tap. Pearson moved on, this time to Bradford, where he wrote one of his most famous songs:

Come, join our Army, to battle we go,
Jesus will help us conquer the foe;
Defending the right and opposing the wrong,
The Salvation Army is marching along.

He wrote a new song every week; when *The Song Book of the Salvation Army* was published in 1953 it contained over 20 contributions from Pearson. His technique was to compress the spiritual mission of the Army into the language of combat and perseverance. Jesus is called upon to give the 'blood-washed army universal liberty'; the Lord to give 'more soul-saving love'; and it is 'the Blood', Pearson writes, 'that Washes White'. There is little in the way of texture to these lyrics, though Pearson is capable of writing emphatically of the joys of Christian belief: 'There's a golden harp in glory'; 'Lead me higher' and — just in case the audience still weren't feeling it — 'Joy, joy, joy, there is joy in the Salvation Army'. There are moments where Pearson's lyrics are touched by the nuance of poetry:

> In white, in white, walking in white;
> He makes me worthy through his blood
> To walk with him in white.

Over the tops of the graves, through the last of the filtered light, I see the octagonal wooden structure that marks out the area where the Dissenter's Chapel stood before it was destroyed by the council in the 1960s. The land has been radically edited here; nettles and undergrowth have been ripped out, leaving a motley assemblage of headstones frozen to the spot. Time seems to stop as I walk off the path towards the headstones. I find Pearson's grave, an elegant grey tablet dwarfed by the Gothic one behind it. A Celtic emblem is situated above the lettering.

WILLIAM JAMES PEARSON

COLONEL SALVATION ARMY

AND FOR MANY YEARS POET

PROMOTED TO GLORY 17TH OCTOBER 1897

AGED 60 YEARS

HE DIED AT HIS POST

'Poet' carries kudos on a headstone. It's a word that can refute the cancelling effect of death, that can connote — and bring — a kind of immortality. To say that Pearson was a poet 'for many years' waters down that claim, suggests that he tried and failed, or that the artform deserted him. If Pearson identified as poet then the headstone should make a stake for that claim.

There are surviving examples of Pearson's page poetry. 'Major Pearson's Life in Rhyme' was published on the front page of *The War Cry* in 1882:

> The year I came to the General's view
> Was eighteen hundred and seventy-two;
> My home was small, my parents poor,
> But of Salvation they were sure.
> My birth took place in Derby town,
> Where long my parents settled down.
> As years sped on, poetic muse
> Inspired the gifts I had to use;
> Alas! The poet's heart was wrong,
> The verse I wrote was comic song

Pearson's intention was always to take the crowd with him. As a result, his poems strive for simplicity in diction and technique. I am not going to find my overlooked G.M. Hopkins or Emily Dickinson in his work and I can't improve upon Herbert Booth's assessment:

> If by a poet is meant a mind great at seizing a microscopic point
> and magnifying that into a mountain of type and rhyme; or one
> profound at the production of metaphors and measures that only a
> few out of every thousand of his fellows can squeeze through mental
> digestions — Pearson was none such as that. If on the other hand
> the power of the poet is to seize the hard facts of life and turn them
> into song, to extract from the commonplace events their melody; to
> fasten upon the great issues of this world and the next, interpreting
> them into language for a million lips to utter, and a million hearts to
> thrill — then Pearson was a poet.

In the western canon, poetry is believed to have been born
from song (with roots back to Sappho's lyre). In many parts of
the world poetry and song continues to merge in what can best
be described as 'verbal art'. Yet lyrics do come with something
that poetry doesn't: musical accompaniment. Poetry needs to
contain all its own music and the 'metaphors and measures' that
Booth describes, within its own language world. While Booth's
definition of poetry does not satisfy the kind of work I am looking
for in the dead of Tower Hamlets Cemetery Park, he is making a
point about Pearson being a *popular* writer, and one who could
find a straightforward way to express complicated experiences of

perseverance and belief, in lyrics that have been memorised by the masses. There is no doubting Pearson's popularity; his funeral was attended by 6,000 people. Five brass bands lead a cortege along Mile End Road to the old Bow Cemetery, as it was called then.

I leave Pearson where he rests, in the darkness and the rain, his headstone as stable in the earth as his reputation is amongst followers of the Salvation Army. I come out through the kissing gate on Hamlets Way. The Victorian monster of St Clement's, a reformed workhouse-cum-asylum now re-compressed into urban flats, dominates the view. Opened in 1874 as a workhouse, it then became a hospital for chronically ill people before being adapted into a psychiatric unit in 1936. It is now a gated residential area, London's first Community Land Trust. The principle tips the scales though not the overall outcome; only 23 families out of 300 who applied could be given a home. Part payment on old heritage.

A man walks past me rattling coins in his pocket, like a reaper ready to buy my soul for a token quid or a single red rose. A graffito on the wall reads OMEN. There are some things you don't want to know about the cemetery, like who closes the main gates? These things need to happen in silence, as part of the night's unspoken code.

§

WILLIAM SPEAKS ———

I'm late for picking my son up from school, running under grey clouds as the rain begins. A sudden wind blows dead leaves from a tree and across my path. The leaves are green, yellow, auburn, red; each has left behind its own testament. Ahead of me is the Ogden's bell tower, a gothic turret built in 1899. *Ogden's Manufactured Tobacco.* I run past the school that my father went to. In autumn I see my dead father playing in the fields that are now covered in tarmac. In no other season can I see him. He lived in a house across from the bell tower and would take target practice with a pellet gun from his bedroom window. The aim was to make the bell ring. I arrive at my son's school and he walks to me, this child of me, veiling the past and the future. He tells me about his day. We walk past the grounds of the tobacco factory; diggers are breaking the ground, laying the foundations for new houses to be built.

*To run. To see. To buy. To own.*

# Poetic Onions

WHEN ONIONS GAVE UP ALCOHOL he was also giving up his addiction to a live audience, but with an ingenious hairpin turn he brought them with him. He began to realise that poetry could allow him to transition into a new daily activity that didn't land him in trouble with the law, but could keep the synapses firing in his brain. For a while he did both, staggering from one public house to another, using his verse to push back at the injustice he saw around him. Whenever he reached the apex of intoxication his instinct was to take something, or someone, down with him — the gutter can be a lonely place. His body soaked up the ullage, a rank doily in a slick of ale. The local bobbies buzzed around him like bluebottles, his ailing frame reflected back in their shining irises. They were the superego to his id, the shadow to his flesh. They were his worst self and better self, the gauze to his cicatrix.

Onions seems to have given up drink as the new century approached. He devised a method for removing the booze from his system, but which still allowed him to keep his drinking arm in action, he simply replaced the gin with twenty cups of tea a day. By this stage he was addicted to a stronger, more addictive substance: poetry. Onions raced towards the next comedic end-rhyme as if his life depended on it.

The moment of Onions's conscious transformation into a poet is documented in the court records, between one conviction and another. On 12th July 1896 *Reynold's Newspaper* wrote:

> William Onions — "Spring Onions," as he is known — stepped into the witness box at Thames Police Court on Friday, and, addressing Mr. Mead, the Magistrate, said, 'Last time before sentencing me you hesitated, and then called me a fool.'
>
> 'The rebuke was not just. Since then I've turned a poet. Some call me a petty poet.
>
> I want to ask you if I lay myself open if I get the following printed:-
>
> Don't call me a fool, Mr Mead. Dash it. Stow it.
> You've oft hit me a knock-out blow;
> You're not o wise — I'll prove and show it

or else you would more mercy show.
Here I was ne'er called that name before,
where I've caused many a tear and a smile.
So, in case you should not see me more,
I'll take a light through this cracked tile.'

When the laughter in court had subsided, Mr. Mead said: 'By printing that I should say you would not be transgressing the law, but I should advise you not to spend your money in that way. In kindness to you I pointed out the folly of getting drunk, and it is very likely I said you were a foolish man to get drunk so often. Stand down.'

This was a coup d'état from Onions. He reads the poem out loud, knowing that the journalists in court would put it into print for him, and to a much bigger audience than he'd ever reach through self-publication.

Onions's story isn't one of immediate salvation by poetry. A few weeks later *The Tamworth Herald* reported another conversation between Mr Mead and Onions. Between Onions' excuses and the judge's lack of understanding of the psychological nature of addiction, the two reach an impasse as regards to the best way forward for Onions's potential rehabilitation:

Mr. Mead said he had received a report from the prison surgeon that Onions was weak minded, but the surgeon was unable to say that he could be dealt with as an insane person.

He (the magistrate) had before him the prisoner's record, so far as that court was concerned and found he had been convicted no less than 160 times, and during that year he had been convicted on four different occasions for drunkenness. In addition he had been convicted of manslaughter and wilful damage, and it was extremely difficult to know what to do with him.

Onions (interposing) said that he suffered from sleeplessness, and while under remand had been given chloral. In the hospital the officials had been experimenting on him.

Mr Mead: Why don't you experiment on yourself?

Prisoner: Give me the chance and I will leave London tomorrow night. There has been a lot of talk about persons curing drunkenness, and I believe the late Canon Farrar expressed an opinion that some children were brought into the world with a bias towards drink. I think I must be one of those.

In my case it is a disease, very like fever.

Mr Mead: I am not going to imprison you, but understand the next time you are brought here and the facts warrant it, I shall require you to be bound over to keep the peace and to find a surety of £20, and in default of so doing, you will have to go to prison for a long time. Try and be manly. You can go now.

Mr Mead isn't prepared to accept that Onions was simply born into drunkenness and criminality. Onions' decision to leave London had already caused problems for other regions, so that was hardly an option. His alcoholic fever was spreading and nobody seemed able to stop it; but just as convict and judge reached this impasse, the embryonic poet was beginning to emerge.

Over the following year Onions prepared a poem for each of his court appearances; he was yet to see the artform as a saviour, more of a tool to further his notoriety. On 14th April 1898 *The Daily News* reported:

"William Onions — usually called "Spring Onions" and "The East End Poet" — against whom it is said there are upwards of 200 convictions, 34 of which have taken place since 1890, was charged at the Thames Police-court yesterday with drunkenness and disorderly conduct.

The following is a verse from a poem entitled, "The New Crusade," written by Onions when serving a sentence in prison.

> Drink ruins lads, shames the maids
> And hurries on the drunkard's doom;
> On home, sweet home, it makes its raids,
> and where love dwelt leaves quite a gloom.
> Strong drink turns a loving heart to stone,
> Severs what once was near and dear.
> Separates some true and loving one:
> Then — too late — flows the bitter tear.

On Tuesday morning Onions, when in a drunken condition, forced his way into the court and, pointing to the magistrate, kept shouting, "I want to speak to that man." He was got outside, where he continued his abusive and disorderly behaviour, and had to be locked up.

Onions now said his object in coming to the court was to ask the magistrate to help him. He only came out of prison on Monday after "doing six weeks" and was suffering from sciatica. He wanted a ticket for the infirmary, and if the magistrate would give him another chance he would thank him for it. Perhaps Mr Fitzsimmons, the missionary, would find him a job. He was willing to go to any part of Ireland, Scotland or Wales, money was a secondary consideration.

Onions' transformation came with an inversion of the usual poetic mould. Many poets have degenerated into malfunction, become so invested in the language worlds they create that they can no longer follow the rules of society. Onions did the opposite; when he gave up drink for poetry, he used his work to celebrate not only his own anniversaries of sobriety but also royal occasions, thereby giving himself a role as social commentator. Some of his poems spread like wildfire through the East End, gaining a popularity that transformed the myth of Onions from a down-and-out to a spokesperson for the national mood.

Despite their lack of literary finesse, Onions' poems show a clear understanding of popular culture. One of the most successful of his poems was written to mark the Coronation of Edward VII in 1902.

> The King, His Majesty, and may him Heaven bless.
> He don't put no side on in his dress.
> For, though he owns castles and palaces and houses,
> He wears, just like you and me, coats and waistcoats and trousis.

Onions was the Pam Ayres of his day, demonstrating an ability to capture what connects people across class (in this case Edward's choice of clothes), displaying a talent for creatively flexing rhyme for comedic effect; here, the cockney-sounding 'trousis' is made to chime with 'houses'.

When Onions gave up drink he risked losing his captive audience. In a final flourish, he decided to make the judge's dock work as his platform for reaching people. This time, however, he wouldn't need to appear as the accused. Each month, from this date on, he appeared at the criminal court to read a poem in honour of the magistrate. This meant that on days when there was little news in court he was guaranteed to get a mention in the newspapers.

Onions returned to the place where he'd appeared so many times without an alibi or witness, only now he was armed with his latest poem. *The Nottingham Evening Post* reported in May 1899 how Onions had returned to the court to tell the magistrate that he had, at last, made a breakthrough.

> "William, or "Spring" Onions, usually known as The East End Poet, waited on Mr Mead at the Thames Police-court yesterday, and said, as that morning was the anniversary of his being a sober man for six months, he had come to let his worship know he intended to continue a sober man.
>
> As all knew, he had been a drunkard for many years, but by swilling

down plenty of tea he had got rid of all taste or longing for alcohol.

Mr Mead: Then tea is a powerful antidote. Your testimony is extremely valuable, considering your experience, and no doubt the medical profession will take notice of it. I am glad to hear you are reforming.

Onions: Yes; tea is the thing, sir. I take four or five pints of it everyday, instead of four and twenty pints of beer.

Onions then gave his worship accounts of the careers of some of his drunken companions, and took his departure, after observing he had two newly-written poems in his pocket.

If Onions had relied on a publisher to bring his work to a readership he might have grown bored, but by swerving the literary gatekeepers he generated a huge audience for his work through the newspapers. Onions continued to be recognised throughout the East End. Thousands of better poets have died in obscurity, believing an audience would come to them; Onions understood mass culture and had an unswerving belief in his place within it. His monthly poem to his Honour became a cultural fixture. The poems were sometimes about the perils of drink and the sadness of wasting a life, but some were also propelled by the inverse: the joys of sobriety. *The Manchester Courier* reported in November 1902:

THE EAST END POET'S FIFTH ANNIVERSARY

At the Thames Police Court "Spring Onions", the East End Poet, waited on Mr. Mead and assured his Worship that if ever a man was happy and joyful that day he was, for it was five years that morning since he became a total abstainer. What was more, he had not got tired of being a teetotaller, and never should be.

He asked the magistrate's acceptance of a poem, in which were the lines

I'm five years teetotal; that's all right, my friend,
Some troubles are blessings robed in disguise,
To make you more careful, prayerful and wise.

Mr Mead said he was very glad to see Onions, and was pleased to hear he was able to persevere in the reform initiated five years ago.

As Onions wrote in another poem, he had 'vowed to fight and conquer frothy grimes'. And then there were the ongoing poems marking royal occasions. Within the dust and stagnation of the living quarters where he was later found dead, a witness found a letter from the Queen of Denmark's Secretary, thanking Onions for a poem that he'd sent to her in sympathy, following the death of King Christian IX. 'Yellowed by time and creased by much handling,' one journalist wrote, 'it was Spring Onions' most cherished material possession, as his glory in his reformation was his greatest spiritual pride.' Having touched the lives of thousands of the poor, and the middle-class readers of the news, Onions began to look upwards to the luminosity of the Royals. On this occasion his gaze had been met. Influence would always be beyond him, but recognition, he found, was attainable. To be briefly heard for his words was worth at least a dozen convictions.

There was something else that poetry gave Onions: evidence. The poems he read to the magistrate were the accrued facts that not only had poetry changed his life, but he was the governing agency behind it. His poems were, and remain, the documentation detailing how he transformed his life from within. But there was another question that he — like every other poet — had to wrestle with: would he be read in the future?

§

WILLIAM SPEAKS ————

As autumn ends, the trees grow visible. From May to August I sat in the same seat, or upstairs at my son's desk, overlooking the gardens on the new estate. Now it's Halloween and the tree in front of me is at last visible. Copper-lit drops of molten ore hang from bare branches, caught in their final stasis. The tree is like a fired God, a net which drags the old world into the new — a snare shared equally between living and dead. On All Hallows, when the living colour their faces with the echoes of the deceased — and linger at unknown doors — every home could belong to us. The tree is a flame welcoming in the burnings that follow: Guy Fawkes lighting up each suburb and communal park. A robin lands in this living god, the tree, and disappears in its auburn rhizomes. This day we pass through once each year.

*To grow. To net. To snare. To pass.*

# On the Case of Uncle Fred

*Yes, here and there some weary wanderer*
  *In that same city of tremendous night,*
*Will understand the speech, and feel a stir*
  *Of fellowship in all-disastrous fight;*
*'I suffer mute and lonely, yet another*
*Uplifts his voice to let me know a brother*
  *Travels the same wild paths though out of sight.'*

B.V. THOMSON, *THE CITY OF DREADFUL NIGHT*

I'M THROWN ANOTHER LEAD by Diane Kendall. She meets me at the Southern Grove entrance, and we sit on a bench to look at the evidence. Frederick Cooper, an East End local known for his wit, could be a poet. As with so many of the poets buried here my only link is through his obituary — which Diane has found — this time from a 1925 copy of the *East London Observer*.

> In the death of Mr. Fredk. Cooper, of Dudley Terrace, Beaumont street, Mile End, another link has snapped in the chain of old residents in East London. The deceased had reached the ripe old age of 81, and until recently had enjoyed fairly good health; but towards the middle of last year, however his might had began to fail, and an

operation for cataract was found necessary, which was not entirely successful and he became nearly blind, an irksome condition for one who had been a great reader, and this deprivation seemed to weigh heavily upon him. A man of many parts, Mr Cooper had travelled extensively, and was well known and held in high esteem by a large circle of friends, especially so in pro-life, where he was affectionately known by all the prominent members as "Uncle Fred". A past-master of raconteur, and his presence at any function was an induction of a happy hour or so, for his criticism and stories always flavoured of real life events dramatically described. The deceased gentleman was also gifted with the pen, and his verse – some of which was published in this journal – on current events, especially so during the late war, have been read and appreciated by many notable and distinguished persons in high office.

Diane has Cooper's plot number archived on her phone and, bracing another summer storm, we walk into the Sanctuary Wood, towards Ivatts and the Charterhouse Graves. Cooper's grave is in a fenced-off woodland that's completely overgrown, an impenetrable patch in which trees are towering with trunks you could build a cabin inside. It's hard to count the graves — it looks inaccessible — but Diane's done this many times before and takes the lead. "Let's try this the old-fashioned way," she says, and looking at the map she counts 37 graves along, then six back, to where Cooper should be buried. According to her map, Cooper's grave hasn't been documented in recent times. The most I can hope for is an empty spot.

*The East London Observer* also reported that in later life Uncle Fred had received some lines from Queen Alexandra, thanking him for a poem written about the men of the Anchor Brewery who had lost their lives in the First World War. This letter would have been in response to Cooper's 'Lest We Forget', published in the same newspaper. The poem has none of the complexity of Howard's 'The Charges' — no sense of the corruption of power and the reality of the trenches — and is written as a straightforward communication of emotion to people of his age.

> Of our young workmates we were proud to tell
> Their answer to their King and Country, loved so well.
> Leaving their peaceful work and homes so dear
> To face a cruel and treacherous enemy always near

In another poem, Cooper makes an assault on William II, in which he states, 'Germany's learnt the lesson, how the brave boys fight'. Despite this, Cooper's poem follows on the same page from a reprint of Wordsworth's poem 'Ode', which ends, 'for the sway of equity renewed / For liberty confirmed, and peace restored!'

Long before Cooper found poetry, he had decided not to continue his father's work at Charrington's Brewery on Mile End Road (Frederick later returned and worked there for 46 years). He chose instead to go to sea, visiting Australia and seeing the first ever test match of cricket while he was there. One time he walked all the way from Liverpool to his father's house, arriving as a 'poor sailor man' — a means of transport that is still one up from my own: the Virgin Pendolino from Lime Street to Euston.

It's worth remembering that Cooper is described for his love of reading, then for his travels, then for his wit, and only after that as a poet. The obituarist goes on to describe his tour of Britain, acting out the role of 'Mikado' in a performance called *A Night in Japan*. He then took up circus work in the Channel Islands. It was during this time that he began to write, including a poem, 'A Trip to Brighton', which documents, in simple rhymed couplets, a trip out to sea:

With lovely weather, our hearts filled with joy
We started away from the "Old Black Boy,"
That noted hostel on the Mile End Road
Where three hundred years or more the record shows

There is such ebullience in Cooper's spirit that it seems curmudgeonly to point out the clunkiness of these lines, that awkward compromising of sense meaning to accommodate the end-rhymes. Cooper actually veers from his own parameter and fails to stick to the form he has set himself; in the third and fourth lines of the poem, 'shows' is attempted to rhyme with 'Road'. This would work fine if his intention was a casual slant-rhyme, but the other lines of the poem end with full rhymes locked together like freshly baked bricks.

As with many poems written for occasions, Cooper's work lapses into archaic ('three hundred years or more the record shows'), a sign that his reading of other poets was limited to older texts rather than what was available in the contemporary poetry of the period. T.S. Eliot's 'Prufrock' for example, with is piercing imagery and deliberate under-cutting of end-rhyme, had been published the year before. Cooper's poem goes on to eulogise the pleasure of good whiskey and 'fine Maidstone Ale', expressing pity for anyone 'condemn[ed] all his life to drink nothing but water'. It is this vitality, rather than the poems, that was celebrated in Uncle Fred's life. I try to conjure that same energy from this silent spot, in all its abundance and lushness.

On the occasion of his golden wedding anniversary in 1922, when Cooper's health was starting to falter, the *East London*

*Observer* covered the festivities and marked out 'that sprightliness and activity which has characterised him throughout his life'. At his burial, the grounds were covered with floral tributes from the hundreds of people who had known him. Over 100 years later the ground is impenetrable with wildflowers and shrubbage. Cemeteries are not fixed places; they grow and slide and mutate. Aspects may be forgotten — as people are, as poets are — but there is always the chance of rediscovery.

I enter into the woodland while Diane stays on the fringe to mark my direction. "Use this urn" as a marker she says, as I wade through great shrubs of nipplewort and bushels of nettles, stepping over mortsafes and rusted metal hidden in the lush undergrowth. I shout the names on the headstones back to Diane so she can check them on her map: Hughes, Smyth, Harrington. Just when I need a string of unusual names to mark the spot all I can find are the English standards. "GEORGE," I shout. "What's his surname?" Diane asks. "GEORGE," I reply, steadying myself against a huge Celtic cross. The night is folding the cemetery into its black lava — we might have 10 minutes until I'm stranded on this shifting island. "HALES," I shout. She replies: "Did you say HALES?" "Yes, HALES!" 'You're three graves away, walk towards me." I walk towards the empty space where I expect Cooper's grave once was, hoping to at least mark the empty spot with the help of the name on the grave next to it. I pull back a plant to read the name on the headstone: FREDERICK COOPER. "I've found him," I shout. "This is it!" Diane's as excited as I am and is coming in to take a look, stepping through the snags and rocky holdfasts. She holds back the shrubs as I photograph the remaining facts of a forgotten poet's life.

IN LOVING MEMORY

OF

FREDERICK COOPER

WHO PASSED TO REST

2ND DECR 1925

AGED 82 YEARS

*"THE EYES OF THE BLIND ARE OPENED*

*AND THE WEARY ARE AT REST"*

ALSO SARAH COOPER

HIS BELOVED WIFE

WHO PASSED TO HER REST

2ND OCTOBER 1926

AGED 74 YEARS

Diane and I leave the cemetery in dark, via the Barnado's memorial, strong, caring hands supporting a Cockney sparrow. As we walk through the dusk I spot another found poem:

No. 9087

FORECAST

1888

For once the rain has passed over. Clear night sky: things are looking good.

§

WILLIAM SPEAKS ————

How can all the lost souls find space in the spirit world? Does Halloween leave room for my personal dead? Do lanterns lit by children momentarily join the orbs of the deceased? Should I be holding the hands of my dead instead of the hand of my son, whose bag is filled with candy and homemade biscuits, gathered from the doors of strangers? My son knocks three times on each door, waits behind his mask, for generosity or lethargy to transmit. There are those who have sellotaped their letterboxes against the wrap of sugar-rushed fingers. A Glaswegian man answers the door, unprepared, and caught out by his absence of treats says, "Ach, sorry, my wife's out." A shadow of a man down an alley, surrounded by children, holds live fireworks up to a distant galaxy. A woman hands us a biscuit made to look like a bloodshot eye. I gather in my dead to hold them for long enough to see them clearly — they flee from me like data.

*To walk. To knock. To Ach. To share.*

# The March of the Cyclops
## —— REHEARSING IN THE CEMETERY

*Then I would follow in among the last:*
*And in the porch a shrouded figure stood,*
*And challenged each one pausing ere he passed,*
*With deep eyes burning through a blank white hood:*
*Whence come you in the world of life and light*
*To this our City of Tremendous Night?*

B.V. THOMSON, *THE CITY OF DREADFUL NIGHT*

WHAT DOES IT MEAN to perform in the cemetery? I'm about to find out. The plans have bigged themselves up into performance dates, budgets, marketing plans, press releases. I've been commissioned by Spitalfields Festival for three events in early December and I need a musician, an actor and a volunteers' steward to make it happen. I'm here again with my publisher, Tom Chivers, to plot out a possible route, only this time we're in the cold. We had watched *Depart* back in the early summer when half-dressed dancers could limber up a sycamore in a faint breeze, then unfurl themselves like ivy until they reached the bottom. Tom and I stand like henchman, angling for a way in, staring at the bare, cracked cemetery and fidgeting with the zips on our thick, black overcoats.

The plan is not only to commemorate the poets buried here but also to build on that with layers of newly created material. We're bringing in a second and third performer: Nick Murray on viola, and actor John Canfield. We're going to make recordings of my own texts and loop them back as audio as the audience walks along the paths. So far so good, but how do we stop ourselves from getting lost in the dark? I could be turning into a sickly creature of the night, a Victorian vapour uncoupled from app culture. I think of that line from *Julius Caesar*: 'Night hangs upon mine eyes; my bones would rest / That have but laboured to attain this hour'. The hour of the performance is coming.

As we walk, the evening of *Depart* seems lost in a previous epoch, an evening scented with wildflowers and tinned lager. After the performance, Tom tells me, there will be mulled wine in the Soanes Centre. Whatever I do here must be opposite to the centrality of the dancers' bodies; the focus instead should be on the words of the dead poets. Those words will be transferred by osmosis, through me, Nick and John — to the audience. Pulse above bracken.

I tell Tom about my theory of seeking dead poets in the dark here being like the one-eyed searching for the one-eyed — a hunt of the Cyclops. For months I've been appearing at the gates of the cemetery like a scarecrow, pockets stuffed with printed-out poems. Shine the single lens of a torch and hope that something glints back.

We move over the crossroads into the Sanctuary Wood, walking through paths strewn with russet leaves. We arrive at the Ash Wood, near where William Sherrard is buried. Tom and I plan for the audience to congregate here at the crossroads. It is a natural place to stop and perform, despite the floor being sodden with platelets of leaves, their individual forms weathering into mulch. Tom takes a photo of me standing on the exact spot, then shows me the photograph. The feeling is of being doubled; a version of the self I recognise stands in green, holding an armful of notes.

We stop and talk ourselves into a future night with an audience. Nick will stand behind the graves — floodlit from below — and play the viola. Then I will appear to make an opening statement in poetic prose. All performers will be wearing black. Torches will guide us from darkness. Floodlights, speakers, LED lights. Tom lives for the fine detailing of live performance. This is a long way from the long, lonely, nights of pulling back brambles in the search for forgotten poets, some of whom I'm still yet to find. As Khaled Khalifa writes, 'Death is Hard Work'. So much of my work on this project has involved digging deep into the layers of the past to write for a future moment that a reader will experience alone, but with this performance I will see the faces of the audiences in the lived moment. We will meet the dead together.

As we walk towards the northern edge of the cemetery, there is the constant shearing sound of our shoes bulldozing the leaves. Above us is the sound of owl wings, crisp as a whip. A huge leaf — perhaps the last of the autumn — lands on a grave with the weight of a leather bag. Our voices, disembodied in the darkness, suggest the best ways to enhance the artifice: "John can maybe hide in the trees there"; "Let's light these graves"; "We liked the idea of the crossroads didn't we?" Paranormal investigators use recordings to capture the sounds and voices of ghosts, making the dead appear stranger than they are. We are planning the opposite: to make ourselves strange in order to bring the dead closer to the living. I just need to prepare the words of the dead for the ears of the live audience. Tom and I talk about the audience as if *they* are the ghosts, invisible at this point, and still to be believed. "So, the audience will come this way?" I ask Tom, who's taking photographs of a deserted plot of land. I make a note of the obelisk that Tom wants me to emerge from. We plan cues. Clarify stage directions. I hear myself say, "Can we practise this moment, it will put my mind at ease?" "Chris," Tom says, "I think you should step into this light."

This is a different incarnation of the project. "My body, my work," I'll begin. "My body of work." John, my twin Cyclops, will respond from distance: "Who is this?" Then give a disembodied shout through the woods. Invisible presences will become embodied in this massive outdoor space — theatre without edges. The cemetery takes Peter Brook's definition of theatre as 'the empty space' to another level. A train whistles as it shuttles past the cemetery, swerving the edge it might have fallen off.

As we plan logistics, a fox walks behind us. Tom flashes a torch. It looks up at us, like Satan tiptoeing to whisper in Eve's ear. It stops. Looks again. Maybe it's our ear it wants to whisper in? But then it's off, its dash of green eyes drowned by the heavy bourbon of the night. We're neither food nor feeders, just two men rehearsing for something that's yet to happen. The two men becomes three. Tom is talking into his phone, giving John Canfield instructions on where to find us. The arrival of our actor suddenly gives the practice run the feel of the real thing.

Tom plans the exact locations for the LED lights which will outline the path for the audience. He places one down for practice; the static flare uplights his face. I stand on the flat stone slab of a monument and am instantly floodlit. Tom tells John to hide in the bushes behind. The comedy of the scenario has the three of us laughing: Carry on Corpsing.

John shouts from behind the bushes: "Do you want me in the dark?" Tom shouts "Yes" then John disappears from view, back into the bushes. I practice my lines: "Is there beauty and dignity in a work of art?" My words seem strange here, voiced outwards into the freezing cold and dark. The rehearsal projects us into future time; we exist in a shared imaginary, envisioning where the audience will stand and where the music will play from. We decide on areas to perform that are close enough to where poets are buried, as if that might draw on their atomised energy — the knowledge that they were, and we are. John and I are the undying Cyclops: two men in black, refusing to look at each other.

What does it mean to rehearse in the cemetery? Looking around me at the cornucopia of graves — the land's exploding basket of memorials — it's clear that we're also rehearsing for something much bigger: the final curtain of our own deaths. Can the artifice of live art really be called life? And if it is, does the rehearsal count? The present feels like an invisible cloak, as if we are here but not truly visible. Our only audience this evening is the dead. Deep breathing in the wings. Final call. Blackout.

With a peculiar feeling of disembodiment I hear myself asking Tom: "We haven't passed our pausing place have we?" The dead have found theirs. Behind us a high-rise tower throws back sepia cubes of light. Something moves in the nearest tree. Tom stops me as I'm reading, tells me to declaim more. We're gearing up, in rehearsal, to visit the grave of Pearson. I need to walk the audience there — and speak the words — with conviction. I tell John that I'm going to rewrite this piece of the script. "I don't know if I'm trying to give facts," I say, "or tell people something about myself." Everything's in flux, even the words of my script. On the night, Nick, our musician, will be looking for my form moving along the path to know when to start playing his viola. Tom suggests that I could reverse my Kindle and hold it to my chest to give him a signal. A block of luminescence; a rectangular orb coded in the darkness.

"There's a fucking stump there," I say to the others as I stumble over a grave. I hear someone say "revenant". A small patch of land that takes seven breezy seconds to walk through in summer light becomes a no man's land of bramble, snag and ditch in darkness. For a moment, I picture us as we will appear on the night: four men dressed in black, measuring and plotting moves around a grave. Resurrectionists of the word. A family of five fly past on bikes, red lights flashing a thousand beats a second. I lift leaves from the ground and let them fall on a flattened headstone; the patina of pending mulch drifts slowly through the freeze. I make my way back to the path where John's waiting, script in hand. We walk through the hysterical sibilants of leaves, then stop to read the monument to those who died in Poplar during the Second World War.

We circle the bottom of the Round Glade, then move along Holly Walk. Over the walls of the cemetery, and then over the railway arches, the tip of Canary Wharf beats like the pulsing heart of a maggot. Tom asks if I'm confident of the direction I'm taking us in? "Yes," I say, "It's easy, just keep walking" — but as I say it, I'm instantly unsure of myself. There's nothing ahead but darkness, no path to follow. All confidence melts from me as we walk into the night. Darkness brings indecision. Tom reminds us that on the night of the performance there will be LED lights to direct us. A corvus rattles its syrinx, disapproving of everything.

Then we're walking again, our shoes scuffing the floor, making the long walk back through Ash Wood to the war memorial and the finale. It's here that the words I read from the *Disembodied Essay* will play back through audio on both sides of the path, the words of the Williams transmitting from hidden sources. I imagine this is how the dead poets will one day signal their resurrection, their words no longer attached to their individual bodies, but projecting into the night air.

John stands on the platform to read Howard's war poem. Tom announces, "Chris will then emerge from behind that obelisk." I will read a poem written in the voices of the dead, who are confused and astonished by the world of textspeak that drifts through the ether above them. "My love we came for this," as Nick's viola fades to nothing.

"This."

§

Henry Vaughan wrote, 'They are all gone into the world of light'. There is a world map in front of me. The sun's flash, through the blinds, sends stripes across its surface. The tree outside has been in consonant chime for hours. Vaughan's much-loved younger brother died, then Vaughan lost his wife. The poet had fought in civil war, suffered physical pain. His saying was 'moriendo, revixi': *by dying, I gain new light*. He wrote the poems in *Silex Scintillians* which made his name. His early light, he said, was blighted with the mist of bad decision.

The stripes across the map pad in shadow, cat's paws moving over South America and Africa. Outside the window the children have been unmoored from schools. Did Vaughan believe, in certain light, he could reach his brother again? And his wife? He put the world of light up *On that hill*. It was the poem, at last, which cleansed the glass.

*To go. To reach. To gain. To fight.*

# The Poet Bloomfield

*Of all things human which are strange and wild*
*This is perchance the wildest and most strange,*
*And showeth man most utterly beguiled,*
*To those who haunt that sunless City's range;*
*That he bemoans himself for aye, repeating*
*How Time is deadly swift, how life is fleeting,*
*How naught is constant on the earth but change.*
B.V. THOMSON, *THE CITY OF DREADFUL NIGHT*

ANOTHER RIDDLE HAS ARRIVED in my inbox. Diane Kendall has sent me an obituary for 'The Poet Bloomfield' (*Shoreditch Observer*, June 30th 1866).

I'm here of an evening to look for his grave, but having something to actually look for has taken some weeks and the help of a taskforce. I began by searching the Tower Hamlets death records for any Bloomfields who were buried here in 1866. I found a Robert Henry Bloomfield who had been buried here a few days before this obituary: aged 59, place of residence Hoxton. This chimes with the obituary. Apart from one thing: how could Bloomfield have had 'daughters' who are older than he was —

THE POET BLOOMFIELD.—His readers still are many, notwithstanding the encroaching partiality for works of proper fiction and sensation; and of those who read him, he is perhaps without exception a favourite. His is the rural and moral muse; and his tales will by some be preferred to his elaborate compositions. His own circumstances were never abundant, and his children have fared worse. Two daughters still survive, one in her seventy-fifth the other in her sixty-fifth year. One is a constant, the other, occupied in serving and nursing her sister, an occasional but acute invalid. Their united income amounts to £34 2s. a year. In addition to the extra cost of medical attendance, they have just incurred that of their last brother's illness and interment. His death took place on the 19th inst at 22, Hoxton-square, and he was buried at Bow cemetery on the 22nd. Upon the whole the case is one of interest and painfulness, such is the extraction, merit, and distress of the poet's daughters. It is now made known, as the knowledge of it may possibly prompt a wish on the part of feeling and Christian persons in this neighbourhood to contribute something towards the relief. If so, the parties themselves may be accessible; or G. W. Burrow, Esq., 33, Richmond-road, Dalston, otherwise Poor-Law Board, Whitehall, and his eminently charitable lady, to whose timely interposition, and judicious measures, by the way, one of the daughters owes her existence at the present moment, as also Mr. Attwood, a resident in the same house with the Bloomfields, are ready to represent them.

aged 75 and 65 at the time of his death? Is this a typo? Had the journalist meant to write 'sisters'? The ground symbolises the muddle, the darkness confirms it. I follow a narrow path which leads off the main track and arrive into dense, unlit woodland. Undulating mounds, Blitz or council-ravaged, lead me into the corner of the cemetery where Bloomfield is buried. The trees part and a momentary orange light from the street makes everything visible. I flinch as wind-blown leaves, like warblers, flit their shadows across the ground.

I looked through poetry databases for a Bloomfield and could only find Robert Bloomfield, the self-educated, labouring-class poet, who experienced great poverty but sold 25,000 copies of his book, *The Farmer's Boy*, first published in 1800. I then fell down the rabbit hole of the Robert Bloomfield Society. Their website includes a chronology of Bloomfield's life; I found that the name of one of his sons was Robert Henry and that he was born in the same year as the Robert Henry buried here. I had initially dismissed this connection but a late evening chat with my wife, Sarah, encouraged me to look more closely at the facts. After Bloomfield died, Robert Henry and his two sisters moved to London to try and make some money. One of the sisters was six years older and the other 16 years older, which confirms that the 'daughters' in the obituary were in fact Robert Henry's sisters.

As the obituary shows, the plan failed. Robert Henry's sisters were still in poverty after their brother died.

Ken has been out looking for a headstone here, unlikely given Bloomfield's poverty. The news by email confirms it.

> I've had a rummage and we only know where the G graves are up into the 1100s, so I have no clear idea where Bloomfield is, sorry.

> I have asked one of our heritage folk who may be able to help, so it's not a complete loss just yet. Sorry.

Against long odds I've come out to kick around in the Pollards and Round Glade on the off-chance of finding something relating to Bloomfield. Maybe one of his father's poems strung up for posterity, ragged by the wind? The late twilight wants none of it — and gives me no clues.

Robert Bloomfield, Robert Henry's father, was five feet tall and a shoemaker. Under the lead of his brother George, he had been encouraged as a child to read the newspaper to everyone in the workshop; it was through this that he had become interested in the poetry section of *The London Magazine* (which is still published today). Apparently Bloomfield could carry up to 100 lines in his head until the opportunity came to write them down. There is a lot to admire in his work. *The Farmer's Boy* roves through the seasons with an attuned eye and excels in descriptive language. However, it's Bloomfield's 'Winter Song' that captivates me most.

Dear Boy, throw that Icicle down,
And sweep this deep Snow from the door:
Old Winter comes on with a frown;
A terrible frown for the poor.
In a Season so rude and forlorn
How can age, how can infancy bear
The silent neglect and the scorn
Of those who have plenty to spare?

Fresh broach'd is my Cask of old Ale,
Well-tim'd now the frost is set in;
Here's Job come to tell us a tale,
We'll make him at home to a pin.
While my Wife and I bask o'er the fire,
The roll of the Seasons will prove,
That Time may diminish desire,
But cannot extinguish true love.

O the pleasures of neighbourly chat,
If you can but keep scandal away,

To learn what the world has been at,
And what the great Orators say;
Though the Wind through the crevices sing,
And Hail down the chimney rebound,
I'm happier than many a king
While the Bellows blow Bass to the sound.

Abundance was never my lot:
But out of the trifle that's given,
That no curse may alight on my Cot,
I'll distribute the bounty of Heav'n;
The fool and the slave gather wealth:
But if I add nought to my store,
Yet while I keep conscience in health,
I've a Mine that will never grow poor.

This is a poem for the belly; it reminds me of one of Shakespeare's songs for his loveable rogues. Bloomfield condenses the whole of the passing seasons into just a few lines. The poem synchs with the passing of summer. It's dark early this evening and there's a chilled edge to the breeze: 'Old Winter comes on with a frown'.

Now I knew that Robert Henry was the son of a poet, but what about the obituarist's claims for him being THE POET BLOOMFIELD? I contact John Goodridge, Emeritus Professor at Nottingham Trent University and co-editor of Bloomfield's *Selected Poems*. John has set 'Winter Song' to music and has lived inside the language of the poem, teasing apart the colloquial inflections. I ask him how the word 'Mine' works in the last line — is this Suffolk dialect for 'mind'?

> 'Mine' I assumed was just RB's ethical, metaphorical version of the coal mines, etc., by which 'the fool and the slave gather wealth'; a mine in the sense of a place from which you can dig out value. But this could be wrong.

> (The other puzzle for me was 'make him at home to a pin' -- which I now know means 'get him drunk'. It is apparently an allusion to a tankard, formerly used in the north, having silver pegs or pins set at equal distances from the top to the bottom: by the rules of good fellowship, every person drinking out of one of these tankards was to swallow the quantity contained between two pins; if he drank more or less he was to continue drinking till he ended at a 'pin'. Which was very hard for a novice, so he would keep drinking and get pissed. Now you know).

I'm glad I do know, but it's the son Robert Henry's poems I'm after, and I ask John if he has come across any? John has a sharp eye for a close reading and his response convinces me that I've been reading the obituary too literally:

> I must say first that I have a niggling worry that he may possibly
> not be a poet. One way of reading the obituary is that the whole
> opening gambit is about Robert Bloomfield the well-known poet.
> By this reading it only actually gets to the son, who has actually
> died, much later in the piece. This interpretation would suggest that
> (being a journalist) the writer has looked for an 'angle'– and found
> a good one: the dead man is the son of a famous poet. The writer
> has then got completely carried away with this in writing it up, and
> eclipsed the son's story with the father's. What do you think? I hope
> I'm wrong!

He is, of course, right, and the mention of Robert Henry's
'daughters' isn't a typo at all; it is written from the perspective of
his famous father, The Poet Bloomfield. Robert Henry *has* been
eclipsed by his father, even into death. Radio static floods in behind
me and I turn to see a Deliveroo cyclist velodroming through the
dark with a speaker attached to his handlebars. I walk further
into The Round Glade. Sounds drift in from the estate: a radio
playing jazz; broken fragments of conversation; the clattering of
plates — the diurnal fades into another night. On this side of
the wall there is nature and the epic void of Bloomfield. I picture
myself above his remains — slight of skeleton like his father —

as a worm moves his DNA a millimetre, bringing him news of a visitor. Living poets, be ready for this kind of silence.

There is one further addition that John can add, a rare evidential treat that can only come about by chance. A few year's ago John bought a copy of *The Farmer's Boy* which contained a handwritten note that he'd forgotten about until our email correspondence. It is written by someone who had actually knew Robert Henry. The name from the obituary momentarily walks out from the grey murk of the 1850s.

> One of Robert Bloomfield's children was for many years a Clerk to Mr. Weir, father of Archy's godfather Archie Weir (now the Reverend Dr. Weir). Their office was at Cooper's Hall in Basinghall Street not many yards from Bell Alley where the poet himself once lived. Bloomfield, Mr. Weir's Clerk, was an elderly man when I knew him and looked just what he really was, a quiet plodding Solicitor's Clerk — he died in Mr. Weir's service. Dr. Weir possesses many interesting papers that once belonged to the poet.

Robert Henry carried his father, and his father's papers, through life, as many sons do. But there's more to it than that. John points me to a letter written by Robert Henry which was published in *The Musical World* in 1844. This reveals him as an interesting, if complicated man, and unequivocally as not having written poetry. Robert Henry consciously distances himself from his father, discusses failed relationships, and becomes an advocate for the young.

I make no pretensions to have any profound knowledge of the world, but it appears to me that works of science or taste of a high order are not practically advanced or supported by any except the higher order of the community ... I am the youngest of the family of Robert Bloomfield, who has been known to the public as a writer of poetry ... I believe myself to be uninfluenced by the desire of being distinguished merely because my father was so; distinction is not a thing to be wished for, for the sake of itself alone; and I differ, naturally, from my father. Without making any comparison or mention of abilities, my tastes — which are for calculation and mechanism — are distinct from his, which were for poetry. He felt the beauties of music as much as any person that I have known, and probably admired the other arts, but without studying the abstruse parts ... Those who would judge my character by looking at his history, would be mistaken; my object is to realize things which he and others would have regarded as impossible, though they would have been much gratified, if I have no doubt, if they had seen them realised. I am thirty-six years of age, and was never married. I believe it to be generally the case that those who are of studious dispositions, or fond of abstract subjects, remain single. Without attempting to discuss the causes of this, I must give it as my opinion, that there is a class of women who think themselves neglected when a boy pays attention to an abstract subject, and who therefore use their influence in such a way as to oppose his advancement in the science. If it is true that they oppose the work during its progress, they have not, I think, any just claim on the fruit when brought to perfection … I should carefully preserve a distinction in favour of those who treat the arts with the respect which is due to them. Moreover, I think that children are more entitled to sympathy than the grown up portion of their own class, not because they are really better in quality, which, of course, there is no reason for supposing, but they are less at liberty, and less likely to have money to spend, and in consequence are incapable of patronizing anything. Their characters are more innocent, their passions less complicated and dangerous, while they are very nearly as competent to enjoy and appreciate music as their elders…

Your's,
ROBERT HENRY BLOOMFIELD
16, St James's Street, Clerkenwell.

Robert Henry then wasn't a poet — nor did he want to be. I can't add him to the small rostrum of Tower Hamlets Cemetery Park poets, but I can hold him up for a moment as the complicated individual he was; one with his own passions and attitudes, and who was intent on walking his own path in life.

The path here leads to no memorial. I am pleased to have extracted something of the man whose remains could be six feet below where I'm standing now. My eyes are alert to everything this evening, but what is there to see? The cemetery is all sound and absence. I tread with caution back to the main path, stepping over a broken branch and half a brick, stopping to look down at a random text which I can barely see in the dark. I crouch to take the clue: MADE THE COLONEL'S WAY. A moth flecks onto my arm, silk-warm and coded, like the touch of a ghost. Bloomfield's place in literature came before him, through his father, but for a moment I have reached for him. Perhaps that's enough. To be reached for by a stranger after death is as rare as literary fame.

§

WILLIAM SPEAKS ————

The bus takes me past the school my father went to. Children climb on ropes which are strung above the ground where the old building once stood. Tyres have been cut in half and the children climb through them. They are given full run of the grass, as well as the playground. One child runs through a sea of red leaves carrying a green globe in his hands. Other children follow, trying to get hold of the globe. In the sky a vapour trail swells, expands into mist, then disappears. I close my eyes and hear the noise; a cacophony of voices meld into my own childhood memories. My father, 15 years dead, had his share of those — just as my son will. The bus takes me past the exposed remains of a pub, the Gregson's Well, crumbling from the roof down, branches growing from the wall. A pub my father drank in, ruined before I had the chance to stand a round of my own.

*To climb. To meld. To trail. To grow.*

# The Republic of Graves

*Around the pillars and against the walls*
*Leaned men and shadows; others seemed to brood*
*Bent or recumbent in secluded stalls.*
*Perchance they were not a great multitude*
*Save in that city of so lonely streets*
*Where one may count up every face he meets.*

B.V. THOMSON, *THE CITY OF DREADFUL NIGHT*

WHAT'S MISSING ON MY JOURNEY is the companionship of a living poet. I feel this more with Tower Hamlets than I did with West Norwood and Nunhead. This cemetery is so much of the community, a crucible for daily living, that it's impossible to fully understand it without talking with a poet who has lived in the area for decades and witnessed its changes. After tracking down Bloomfield to a silent corner, now is the time to find a poet to walk with. I'm after someone with an appetite for walking and looking, who might invite me see the place from another angle. My only caveat is that they can't be called William; the dead poets here are leading me down dead ends.

Then I remember a line from poet Stephen Watts: 'I

decided at age eighteen not to take the driver's seat' — opting instead to walk through the East End. I drop him a line. Here's a poet whose work I've admired for many years and whom I've come to know through his visits to the National Poetry Library. I have an intuition — like the first stirring of a poem — that Stephen is the kind of outsider figure who can bring me closer to the poetic history of Tower Hamlets Cemetery Park.

In the falling dusk, Stephen arrives at the Southern Grove entrance like a solar deity, his white beard illuminated under the dark cowl of London sky. It's a strange reality of contemporary poetry that the writers whose work is the most vital — urgent and connected to political and socio-economic realities — are often the most overlooked. Too many poets have never learnt to look outwards. I've heard of workshops being given to young poets in which the tutor gives advice on what poets should be paid to perform at Glastonbury. Outside the window of the workshop the city moves in light — the matter for visions. While so many poets are jumping into their identity coracle and sloshing about on the rapids, canoeing down the swampy middle stream of poetry, netting prizes and residencies as they go, there are poets who quietly work, grafting their own nuances of style and inflexion, taking their reward as the next poem. It's become a commonplace for poetry judges to focus on a poet's 'affirmation of identity', as if that's all there is; to reach for books that can be explained in a sentence — as if that's what makes them worth talking about. All the while, those who care for the essence of the stuff — the flickers of syntax and unique stylistics — go unnoticed. Or worse: become *known* as an overlooked poet. There are too many people on a mission to make poetry exciting without learning to talk about exciting poetry.

Stephen's work documents the East End as a complete sensory experience. It is a tactile, lyric poetry that is the result of walking, touching, listening. His work maps out the eastern edge then folds the map, making the fringes the centre, as it is for those who live here.

We step up into the war memorial and Stephen conjures a ghost he's very used to talking and walking with: the poet Isaac Rosenberg. I remember a line from one of Stephen's poems which describes Rosenberg 'alive in Stepney still ... / on the Mile End Waste'. "Rosenberg was such a wonderful poet for me," Stephen says. "He lived in Whitechapel, lived in eight or nine different places, which shows how financially insecure his family were." I ask Stephen why he has always felt close to Rosenberg? "I think it was because he had Yiddish hidden behind his English," he says. "He spoke Yiddish at home, and the inflections with which he wrote English seemed to have another language behind it. He wrote

English in a very rich and idiosyncratic way." Stephen argues that Rosenberg could have played a part in humanising the narrative of Modernism. He throws the question out to the cemetery: what might have happened if Rosenberg had lived? Stephen suggests we would have had a healthier line of Modernism; Rosenberg would have muffled Eliot's microphone with the scuff of his raincoat. Back in his early days in the East End, Stephen met Rosenberg's friend Joseph Leftwich. From that point on Stephen has documented the poetics of the Yiddish East End, meeting (and later translating) Avrom Stencl, 'the poet of Whitechapel'.

As we walk through the Lodge Wood, I ask Stephen what drew him to east London in the first place? In the early '70s Stephen dropped out of university without a degree and 'dropped in' to a life as a shepherd in North Uist, on the Scottish islands. His job was to keep count of sheep across the fields and hills. When he returned to London his instinct for observation came with him and — at a time when high-rise buildings were left unlocked — he intuitively found himself walking to the top floor to see the city from different perspectives. Odd geometric anachronisms of Victorian bricks and 1980s stonework, connected by destitution, and by wildlife. Stephen found that the high-rise blocks were the perfect location to view migrating birds, and from there he began to form his own vision of the East End. It runs through his work like a watermark. As he talks, he holds his glasses at his shoulder, with the same hand on a rucksack of books. With his other hand he conducts his words, gesturing out across the open space, then back to pinch at his beard, in thought: "It's a funny and difficult balance," he says, "being a poet."

Stephen first visited Tower Hamlets Cemetery Park in 1974. He was living in Stratford at the time and he would jump on the 25 bus, feeling himself drawn to the East End, where he would get off — wherever — and walk — wherever. His wife was teaching English to recently arrived Bangladeshi children. He remembers vividly the incredible older women of Tower Hamlets: nurses, teachers, garment workers.

I tell Stephen that I've not found any female poets in Tower Hamlets Cemetery Park. "I'm not surprised," he says. "It's all linked to class. But there must be poets here who we just don't know about." Stephen describes The Basement Writers in Cable Street, organised by Chris Searle, which gave a platform to previously unheard of poets such as Gladys McGee and Sally Flood. "There was a tremendous sense of community back then," Stephen says. "I was reading Rimbaud constantly. I'd jump off the bus and Rimbaud would be going around my head in English translation, and somehow wherever I jumped off it seemed to fit. *Illuminations* seems so much of that time for me."

Walking at night with Stephen reminds me of how many of his poems are filled with vivid dream imagery. The opening poem in his collection *The Blue Bag* (2004) begins: 'Lord in dream I was lifted out of London'. His experience of having lived through the East End in the '80s might explain why the alternative reality of dreamscapes provides the perfect escape from the raptors of 'development'. These are poems which stitch together imagery and rhythm, poems that flex with the details of walks through the lacquered, condensed streets of the city. Anyone who's seen Stephen read his poems knows the force of linguistic energy that comes from his use of propelled speech-rhythms. Sibilants and assonance work like pistons to move his poems forwards. In 'Fieldgate Streets' the East End is captured in descriptive and compressed images.

> Windows of halved betel, of limes
> and coriander and various chillies,
> windows of crushed coffee bleating
> in the deep blue of Aldgate night

The Mile End Waste becomes a motif in Stephen's work. Today, this strip of land is covered with bare trees and boarded-up shops. Stephen's interest — as with the ghost of Rosenberg —

is in channelling the energy of the dead. The Mile End Waste was a place where activists congregated. William Booth gave his first open-air sermon here. This is Stephen's Waste Land — the antithesis of Eliot's bankers walking up King William Street — where Socialists and workers stood up to resist the power structures. Stephen bends down at the Linnell grave in front of us and reads the headstone which includes a quote from the Morris poem. "Cable Street," he says, cryptically, and I know what he's talking about; Stephen connects the riots Linnell was involved in with the 1936 Battle of Cable Street. This was another East End demonstration in which the police used horses as a means of force. This is just the kind of fusion of events that Stephen thrives on.

Sometimes Stephen's visions of the dead are so vivid he asks himself, in the poem, if he's dreaming. The imagined barriers between writing, walking and dreaming are fluid. If, as Thomas Nashe argues, 'a dream is nothing else but the echo of our conceits in the day', then it stands to reason that both dreaming and waking will feed back into the poetry — one across to the other — on a perpetual loop. As Stephen puts it in one poem, 'I can / sit on the top stair dreaming — / which is to say writing'. In Stephen's work, dreaming, writing, walking and resisting all coalesce in a gyration of language that refuses to comply with the status quo. The well-known tactic of the underclass is carried through to the stylistics of the poems themselves: keep moving and the bastards can't grind you down. In this tension between 'reason & energy', as Stephen puts it in a paraphrase of Michael Hamburger, the poems move as if in a 'slow dance'. This is what poems can be; not static blocks communicating a feeling or idea, but a *movement* before the reader or listener in which resistance is played out in real time — again and then again — each time the poem is enacted.

Stephen stops to smell a strange, alien-like plant that's weeping a sharp, lilac scent. His poems refuse to fit within the parameters of prevailing styles and movements — neither the knotty abstractions of the Cambridge school nor the strait-jacket of the workshop; neither the tenuous application of American vernacular nor the puns and wordplay of the New Gen. Stephen's work is that increasingly uncommon thing today: poems of feeling and of resistance. They amount to a collective threnos for the people and heritage of the East End. Stephen is a poet who can handle enjambment like a violinist, rolling lines over and over, and who has introduced a subtle stylistic to his verbal landscape: the truncated and indented final line. Even the long poems — a shorthand for boredom for many poets — leave you wanting more. As the rain starts, Stephen puts on a grey beanie. He is slim, supple and walks easily in this landscape he's visited many times before — stepping carefully across the wreckage of the land, negotiating his steps between broken stones and ditches.

I ask him about *Republic of Dogs / Republic of Birds* (2016), his auto-fiction that documents the sacking of London's Docklands by rabid developers. Stephen's book chimes with the way the communities of the area have been moved, silenced and side-lined since the 1980s. The manuscript itself was lost (like so much of the community) and then re-found 20 years later.

During this timeframe the remains of the Port of London — parts of which are just over two miles from the cemetery — were homogenized into a Tory playground. Initially conceived by Michael Heseltine as he took a flight over the Thames, Docklands was created as an 'enterprise zone' for investment. In reality this saw historic heritage destroyed and the residential communities pushed out to make way for identikit buildings such as One Canada Square. London became a city of two financial centres, with Docklands the pulsating pacemaker viewable from budget flights. Stephen writes:

> What war had hit this place? ... Shipwright House coming down. Gunners Wharf burnt to its shell. Andrewes House pulled apart. And memory falling in amongst itself, a scoured heap of breeze blocks, human bricks and veins.

Stephen's book was written in the period between the Victorian buildings being ripped down and the new towers yet to rise and claim the light — 'a reversed archaeology'.

Stephen points out across the cemetery and tells me this was once all open land leading down to the river. The cemetery has contained and preserved some of it, but Canary Wharf now dominates everything the eye can see, a Cyclops in the East End's back garden. The final paragraph of the book is composed of just four words in parenthesis, which brings these strands together with incredible force:

'(Unwritten. Mislaid. Or lost)'.

We arrive at the grave of William Ivatts. The text-layer of the memorial is separating from the crumbling stone beneath, flaking away like a sermon written on rice paper. As we approach the grave Stephen says that he'd thought the name 'Ivatts' was 'Watts'. I'm reminded of *A Christmas Carol* when Scrooge is shown his own headstone: 'Are these the shadows of the things that Will be, or are they shadows of things that May be, only?'

In Stephen's work, the library symbolizes the highest and most egalitarian values of a society. The cormorant is presented as a symbol of both perseverance and frailty under corporate pressure:

> That the race to modernity be not measured by the coming of
> subways or skyscrapers, but by the speed with which the sprightly
> grasses push up from the city's stones. And so this sudden presence
> of cormorants in the neon city and in its black night spaces means
> the possibilities of a changed new world.

*The Republic of Dogs* is a book of the reality apocalypse that was
Thatcherite Britain, but an apocalypse in which the people refuse
to zombify — they resist, refuse to lie down. We've passed through
the ever-darkening central section of the cemetery, past a series of
small, low graves. Stephen's ahead of me, dexterous, crouching to
read the details on a small headstone. With his jeweller's eye for
text, he's spotted that each of the graves has a burial from 1951.
In the year of the Festival of Britain, a celebration of peace and
progress, a heavy number fell into the earth here. 'A Tonic for the
Nation' was poured out on the South Bank — along with the
pink fizz — but not everyone made it to the river that summer.
One of the graves is that of a child, and despite the death being
nearly 70 years ago, petunias have been placed in a vase. Signs of
still-living relatives of the dead, theoretically brothers and sisters.
We stop at an area of earth made raggedy by the Blitz and stare at

a flat memorial that's been exploded from within by a rising tree. The name on the grave is ALEC OAKLEY.

We walk through a dense woodland where signs of the homeless of Tower Hamlets are all around. A tipi has been made from sticks. I stop Stephen along Hamlet's Way and point out another of the many eroded headstones that can be read as found poems; this one just a single word with a date:

RHIND
1872

We both read it as RHINO. Then Stephen spots another; this time it's a headstone with atomized text, projecting across white space like one of Edwin Morgan's Emergent poems:

O

  AS

MAY

YEA  S

We walk past the grave of Mary and Robert Lusty, who DEPARTED THIS LIFE in 1902 and 1903 respectively; the stone is now a grey-white slab covered with a surface film of moss.

The fullness of night is around us and Stephen wants to show me the link to his friend, Max Sebald, author of *Austerlitz* and other works of dream-collage. In Sebald's novel the central character, Jacques Austerlitz, lives near the Jewish Cemetery in Stepney Green, but ends up in St Clement's Asylum following a nervous breakdown. Sebald wrote this between 1996 and 2001, during the period when Stephen would walk with him around Whitechapel and Stepney. Sebald absorbed the atmospherics of the streets, led by Stephen's deep knowledge of the place combined with a compulsion for getting lost anew each time.

A low-flying plane sucks up the silence as it rises from City Airport. Stephen walks ahead, under the hood of the woodland. The problem is that four paths converge at the centre, and in the darkness each one looks the same. Stephen is up ahead, shoes grinding gravel, on the hunt for the granite signifiers of the location he wants to show me. A few minutes ago we were talking about Sebald's intention to make the reader lost. Now we *are* lost. I hear Stephen say, "I'm not exactly sure where I am", but I can't see him, his white hair swallowed into the night. A few minutes later he reappears: "We're looking South". I lose sight of him again, but can still hear him walking quickly through the grounds, on the hunt for an angel.

Stephen stops just a few graves down from William

Sherrard, the self-declared 'Bromley Poet'. We're looking at the pedestal of a grave. An angel is wedged into the earth next to it. The memorial which was once on the pedestal is now on the floor, and on the other side of the angel is a slab of black granite — laid flat on its side — with the name HENRY JAMES cut in gold. Stephen opens a copy of *Austerlitz* and I shine my torch on the page. The photograph in the novel is of this exact spot, only this version shows the angel on top of the pedestal and the HENRY JAMES memorial facing the other way, resting on the pedestal, with the text upside-down. "I think Sebald chose this grave because he loved Walter Benjamin, because of the angel, and then there's Henry James, and he put that in — not as a hugely serious point — but he liked doing things like that. It's possible it was by chance, but it's unlikely." Standing here, looking at a photograph of the exact same location, conjures an odd doubling effect, an uncanny ghosting of the self. "It's odd," Stephen says. "Someone's turned the Henry James grave around and displaced the angel." The angel stands upright from the loam now, removed from its solid base in Sebald's photo, its arms broken off.

The rain is falling. I put up an umbrella with one hand and shine the torch from my phone with the other. We agree that Stephen should read from the novel. I can feel the weight of St Clement's behind us, a mass slowing down time — the deep bunker of Austerlitz's crisis.

Imperceptibly, the day had begun drawing to a close as Austerlitz talked, and the light was already fading when we left the house in Alderney Street together to walk a little way out of town, along the Mile End Road to the large Tower Hamlets cemetery, which is surrounded by a tall, dark brick wall and, like the adjoining complex of St. Clement's Hospital, according to a remark made by Austerlitz in passing, was one of the scenes of this phase of his story. In the twilight slowly falling over London we walked along the paths of the cemetery, past monuments erected by the Victorians to commemorate their dead, past mausoleums, marble crosses, stelae and obelisks, bulbous urns and statues of angels many of them wingless or otherwise mutilated, turned to stone, so it seemed to me, at the very moment when they were about to take off. Most of the memorials had long ago been tilted to one side or thrown over entirely by the roots of sycamores which were shooting up everywhere. The sarcophagi covered with pale green, grey, ochre and orange lichens were broken, some of the graves themselves had risen from the ground or sunk into it, so that you might think that an earthquake had shaken this abode of the departed, or else that, summoned to the last judgement, they had upset, as they rose from their resting places, the neat and tidy order we impose on them. In the first few weeks after his return from Bohemia, Austerlitz continued his tale as we walked on, he had learnt by heart the names and dates of birth and death of those buried here, he had taken home pebbles and ivy leaves and on one occasion a stone rose, and the stone hand broken off one of the angels, but however much my walks in Tower Hamlets might soothe me during the day, said Austerlitz, at night I was plagued by the most frightful anxiety attacks which sometimes lasted for hours on end.

In Sebald's book, Tower Hamlets cemetery is ground zero, a mutilated and mutated landscape where the fractured living find solace in the dead. For Austerlitz, feelings of annihilation and 'mental absence' are soothed as he walks through the grounds during the day. As we stand in the dark, two poets under a sodden umbrella, I think that Sebald might have had Austerlitz walk here of a night. Tower Hamlets Cemetery Park as an antidote to anxiety. As Stephen reads, he moves to the rhythm of the text, counterpointed by falling rain. Stephen finishes reading and points at the angel: "It looks like someone has taken the angel down," he says, "so it can't rise up."

We walk out of the cemetery onto Hamlet's Way, intent on tracking down the geometric monster that is St Clement's Hospital. Stephen walks to one of the arched doorways in the residential community and looks through the iron gates, which have an electronic access point attached to it.

We then follow the edges along Brokesley Street, looking over the 12-foot wall. "It looks like a cross between a hospital and a prison," Stephen says. "I can't quite shake that off. As if hospitals aren't meant to be places of comfort at all." The building is a conundrum; sections stand alone, like self-contained towers. There might be something in the architecture based on Jeremy Bentham's Panopticon principle, security's divide and rule; keep the inmates in view, sub-divide and contain them in different parts of the building so they can't congregate and collectivise. Regulated rows of windows look down over the cemetery wall. Stephen knows poets who have spent time in St. Clement's. One of them actually benefitted from his spell inside. As he talks, Stephen throws a hand back to the cemetery: "There must have been poetry by people in the workhouse, but how much of it was kept and written down? We walk along the graves and all the parts where there are no graves, and there must have been poetry from those people, but you can only say that, you can't document it."

We walk along Mile End Road, like thousands have done before, in search of beer. The Bow Bells has the biggest pub windows in London, an observatory looking out to the traffic. At the bar we realise we share a passion for Blue Moon Belgian White. We talk poetry. By the time we leave we're in a fine, generative drizzle, mildly blurred with good beer. At Bow station I notice the map for the 'night tube' and see that Mile End is listed as one of the stations now open for nocturnal travel. I picture the four dead Williams boarding the train in the lag between exhausted revellers and morning commuters, poems in hand like takeaway flyers. Stephen's train arrives and I step away as the doors close on our handshake. He disappears in transit towards Shadwell, just one stop — and then a few steps — to the river that first drew him here.

A few weeks later Stephen emails me with the fruits of our walk, a new poem celebrating the living and evoking the dead poets of Tower Hamlets Cemetery Park; a siren calling the dead up from the ground.


*Lost Poets My East End*


Who were they ?
The lost poets of my East End
Corporal Herbert Ernest Howard
& the death song of Albert Linnell
(Knocked dead by a police horse
Poverty must be met by force)
Better shut up, do no good at all

The poet Sherrard who left nothing
Can be traced but his own epitaph
And a slight chit for his leery wife
The poet Bloomfield father & son
Whose was a rural & moral muse
Or William Spring Onions buried
Nearby in some untasked grave
Two hundred convictions & more
Turning life round on poetry & tea
Who were they ? The last lost poets
Lain up the cemetery of my East End ?
Isaac Rosenberg dead on the Somme
All the women who wrote on scraps
Paper thrown on the midden heaps
All the women before Gladys McGee
& Sally Flood who had to throw their
Woven words in the sinks & latrines
David Kessel with his ruby courage
John Zammit & Howard Mingham
David Amery, Shadwell & Nazrul Naz
Stephen Watts who's certainly lost it.
Who are they ? The lost poets of our
East End, Friends of East End Loonies.

Those buried from the workhouse or
Sent out from St. Clements in sanity
Matchstick Girls & Yiddish Bundists
Avrom Stencl & Mejer Bogdanski
Buried elsewhere & no longer here.
Where are they ? The lost poets !
The last lost poets of my East End !
Eating cheese cake buns in the ABC
Eating biryani in the Sweet & Spicy
Eating fish curry in Garam Bangla
Eating hot beigels in midnight fury
In the violence of a maimed laugh
With the calmness of a slain horse
With the pain of a betrayed voice
With the yeast of a scalped curse
O quietly, listen to their glory …


(Stephen Watts, 20th July 2019)

§

WILLIAM SPEAKS ———

Between London Euston and my station there is so much flat land to cover. I listen to my interview recording with the poet. Back in his house the questions have yet to really begin. A car passes outside his window. That day so planned, so focused; then the motes of dust around us as we prepared to talk. Why do the silent pauses interest me more than the speech? When we'd finished, the poet drove us to the mudflats along the Cumbrian coast, we found what seemed to be the broken hull of a boat but might have been a door. Across the sea we could see Dumfries. The poet tells me that priests on that coast were once so attuned to the landscape they could lock themselves away and still know the time of day. He told me of a Roman charm he's found here, a carved dog with a huge phallus. A talisman or token of love. In these wild spaces, he said, you find out so much about the self.

*To type. To plan. To laugh. To tune.*

# *And So Died a Poet*
## — THE LEGACY OF ONIONS

*He scarcely can believe the blissful change,*
  *He weeps perchance who wept not while accurst;*
*Never again will he approach the range*
  *Infected by that evil spell now burst:*
*Poor wretch! Who once hath paced that dolent city*
*Shall pace it often, doomed beyond all pity,*
  *With horror ever deepening from the first.*
   B.V. THOMSON, *THE CITY OF DREADFUL NIGHT*

I AM STANDING ABOVE THE COMMON GROUND where Onions is buried. Night has started early today: overcast London, twilight since lunch. According the Met Office the sun should be setting at 9.30pm, but the light's been disintegrating in grey clods for hours. A man in shorts has misjudged it and is walking quickly through the cemetery; the turn-ups at his knees show orange legs baked from a real sun, out there somewhere, but now he's looking for a coalface. He pulls a baseball cap over his eyes and keeps walking.

For one who had lived at the centre of society, who craved spectacle, Onions died the way of many older men of the time:

alone, behind his own front door, in a room in Ratcliffe. *The Monmouth Daily Atlas* reported his death in November 1916. Onions hadn't been seen for three days.

The "bobby" sent for the official known as the guardian of the poor, and the guardian broke in the door. There lay Spring Onions on the floor unconscious and dying. He breathed his last before a physician could be summoned. And so died a poet. There was an inquest, at which the coroner gathered enough information to fill out a report reading: "Name, William Onions; age, 84; cause of death senility," and a few other essential but unimportant facts, such as a 5-pound note, £4 in gold and some smaller pieces of money were found in the room. The proceedings were hurried thru, but once they were halted long enough for a neighbour of the old man to explain that he had found tacked to the door behind which Onions lay dying the following verse, under caption of "Every Man His Own Policeman:"

'Keep out of my room, or 'tis my belief,
At the Thames police court you'll come to grief.
Herein is my Temple, wherein I oft pray,
Keep me from temptation and Its accursed way;
My God and my father, I amen say,
Now, octopuses, with hearts of stone.
Leave me and my belongings alone.'

It was Spring Onions' last "poem," and so niggardly is fame it is the only one preserved to posterity. But it was only one of hundreds which the East End poet wrote.

I walk past two men sitting on a bench. They are both wearing fashionable West End clothes and talking to each other over a soundtrack. The smell of marijuana rises like a '60s crematorium. One tells the other that he's been bitten twice, it's throbbing, but he didn't feel it when it happened. Mosquito or vampire? I zip up my collar. The night has come.

Sometimes, when excavating the life of a dead poet, a posthumous gift comes along, and with Onions we have one. The writer Thomas Burke wrote about the different communities and the eccentrics of the East End. His collection of short stories *Limehouse Nights* (1916) documented the poverty in east London and the Chinese community of Limehouse. Burke saw himself as a seer who used an occult process to represent the lives of 'others'. In *Out and About London* (1919), he goes out on a limb to make the case for Onions the poet.

I met "Spring" (privately, Mr. W. G. Waters) once or twice at Stepney. He was a vagrant minstrel of the long line of Villon and Cyrano de Bergerac. His anniversary odes were known to thousands of newspaper readers. He was the self-appointed Laureate of the nation ... Not to know Spring argues yourself unknown. He might have stepped from the covers of Dekker's *Gull's Hornbook*. He was a child of nature. I can't bring myself to believe that he was born of woman. I believe the fairies must have left him under the gooseberry no, under the laurel bush, for he wore the laurel, the myrtle, and the bay as one born to them. He also, on occasion, wore the vine-leaf; and surely that is now an honour as high as the laurel, since all good fellowship and kindliness and conviviality have been sponged from our social life. We have been made dull and hang-dog by law. I wonder what Spring would have said about that law in his unregenerate days – Spring, who was "in" thirty-nine times for "D. and D." He would have written a poem about it, I know: a poem that would have rung through the land, and have brought to camp the numerous army of Boltists, Thresholdists, and Snortists.

Burke offers a fascinating link between Onions and another of the dead poets I've located in the Magnificent Seven. In *Cenotaph South*, I'd written about Nunhead Cemetery's Albert Craig, the 'cricket rhymester'. In *Out and About London*, Burke identifies Onions and Craig with the 'freak poets' of the beginning of the century. They were both, it seems, lauded character poets who had slipped outside the mainstream to capture the public imagination. These are poets who couldn't wait to let their poems do the work for them, poets whose physical bodies were part of the contract with their audience. They needed to be present, delivering poems by voice as couriers of their own language worlds.

> Now the race of London freaks seems ended. Craig, the poet of the Oval Cricket ground ; Spiv Bagster ; the Chiswick miser ; Onions and Robertson ; all are gone. Hunnable is confined ; and G. N. Curzon isn't looking any too well. Even that prolific poet, Rowbotham, self-styled "the modern Homer", has been keeping quiet lately.

Burke recounts paying the ageing poet a visit in his Ratcliffe lodgings.

> Oh, Spring has been one of the boys in his time, believe me. But in his latter years he was dull and virtuous; he kept the pledge of teetotalism for sixteen years, teetotalism meaning abstention from alcoholic liquors. This doesn't mean that he wasn't like all other teetotalers, sometimes drunk. The pious sages who make our by-laws seem to forget that it is as easy to get drunk on tea and coffee as on beer; the only difference being that beer makes you pleasantly drunk, and tea and coffee make you miserably drunk.

> I visited Spring just before his death in his lodging—lodging stranger than that of any Montmartre poet. The Thames Police Court is in Arbour Square, Stepney, and Spring lived near his work. Through

many mean streets I tracked his dwelling, and at last I found it. I climbed flights of broken stairs in a high forbidding house. I stumbled over steps and unexpected turns, and at last I stood with a puffy, red-faced, grey-whiskers, stocky old fellow, in a candle-lit garret whose one window looked over a furtively noisy court.

It was probably his family name of Waters that drove him to drink in his youth, since when, he has been known as the man who put the tea in "teetotal." In his room I noticed a bed of nondescript colour and make-up, a rickety chest of drawers (in which he kept his treasures), two doubtful chairs, a table, a basin, and bits of food strewn impartially everywhere. A thick, limp smell hung over all, and the place seemed set a-jigging by the flickering light of the candle. There I heard his tale. He sat on the safe chair while I flirted with the other.

It was on the fortieth occasion that he yielded to Sir John Dickinson's remonstrances and signed the pledge, and earned the respect of all connected with that court where he had made so many appearances. All through that Christmas and New Year he had, of course, a thin time; it was suffocating to have to refuse the invitation: "Come on, Spring—let's drink your health!" But what did Spring do? Did he yield? Never. When he found he was thirsty, he sat down and wrote a poem, and by the time he had found a rhyme for Burton, the thirst had passed. Then, too, everybody took an interest in him and gave him work and clothes, and so on. Oh, yes, it's a profitable job being a reformed vagabond in Stepney.

He was employed on odd messages and errands for the staff at Thames Police Court, and visited the police-stations round about to do similar errands, such as buying breakfast for the unfortunates who have been locked up all night and are about to face the magistrate. Whatever an overnight prisoner wants in the way of food he may have (intoxicants barred), if he cares to pay for it, and Spring was the agile fellow who fetched it for him; and many stray coppers (money, not policemen) came his way.

All these things he told me as I sat in his mephitic lodging. Spring, like his brother Villon, was a man of all trades; no job was too "odd" for him to take on. Holding horses, taking messages from court to station, writing odes on this and that, opening and shutting doors, and dashing about in his eightieth year just like a newsboy—Spring was certainly a credit to Stepney. On my mentioning that I myself made songs at times, he dashed off the following impromptu, as I was falling down his crazy stairs at midnight:—

Oh, how happy we all should be,
If none of us ever drank anything stronger than tea.
For how can a man hope to write a beautiful song
When he is hanging round the public-houses all day long?

What really comes through the writing here is the depiction of Onions as a swollen, red-faced piece of Stepney, a living synecdoche of the East End. Burke throws a curveball: Onions' real surname, he writes, is Waters. I have since read another, apocryphal source that claims that Onions was given his name due to his love for eating raw spring onions. In *London Labour and the London Poor* Henry Mayhew writes:

> The relish for onions by the poorer classes is not difficult to explain. Onions are strongly stimulating substances, and they owe their peculiar odour and flavour, as well as their pungent and stimulating qualities, to an acrid volatile oil which contains sulphur. This oil becomes absorbed, quickens the circulation, and occasions thirst.

These late findings throw some doubt on the records relating to the child William Onions found in the workhouses. I've tried to track a William Waters to no avail. By the time Onions reached his 30s he was irrefutably known as William 'Spring' Onions. Whether he got that name from birth or through dietary habit we'll never know. The birth records are just one form of documentation, and if it wasn't for his all-pervading character — and his poetry — he would be forgotten.

As I walk along the common ground, night amplifies

the sounds of the gravel. Shoes scrape like a Giallo soundscape. Rain. Pindrops at first, then oddly icy drops. White sparks in the darkness. A train that's just left Limehouse and heading for Stratford clatters ahead with purpose.

As for Onions's legacy, he lives — and will continue to live — by the reputation of *how* he lived, including his radical transformation from a life of crime to law, tea and poetry. The bats are tobogganing around my head, as if in agreement. By the time poetry arrived through Onions's bloodstream, pulsating to his consciousness, he had found a place back in society. We have this transformation documented in newspaper reports, myth and a few surviving poems. We read them to confirm the facts of a life that seems implausible, not because they fire our synapses through language. One of Onion's judges, the right honourable Mr Dickinson, summed up the potential legacy of Onions's work appositely. Having heard Onions recite a poem in the court to celebrate eight years of sobriety, the judge 'did not say what he thought of the composition, but hoped to receive Onions on a similar occasion for many years to come'.

The land peaks into a bank of dry earth, the result of the cemetery's transformation into a park. Onions is believed to be under a path that is lined on each side with crumbling memorials. As an intern in the common ground, Onions' remains lie below, without headstone. This small hill, with a path running over it, leads visitors over his plot. Not for Onions the quiet life. Further into the surrounding grassland, tiny First World War graves appear like toadstools. They seem to rise as I walk. The 'Villon of the East End' was too old to fight in the war, and too poor to be fitted with a headstone, but he has one thing that most of the thousands buried in the common graves don't have: a place in my canon. In addition to the many excellent writers I have uncovered in the Magnificent Seven, I am building a pantheon of eccentric, outsider poets.

When I was here with Ken, he told me that if we were to dig down through this mound of earth we might find Onions' name on a common grave.

In the dark of night, the legacy of the man still radiates.

§

WILLIAM SPEAKS ————

There is a day, once a year, when all seasons can be seen at once. It arrives unexpectedly in autumn. The last juice of summer dies on leaves, turns red, then umber. Plants show their preparedness for spring. As if building an abundance of new fruit, the last on the vine swells, then bursts. Insects and mammals turn to sleep. The robin lands, listens, hops, stares — as it did in summer. I find myself in the cemetery on this day, living fully I think, entranced by a future death. The sun lands inside a wooden birdcage. I do not meditate. I stare, here at the end of the time of embers.

*There is a day, once a year.*

# To Seek the Ghost and Thereby to Wrap It

*This was the festival that filled with light*
*That palace in the City of the Night.*

B.V. THOMSON, *THE CITY OF DREADFUL NIGHT*

THE COLD'S ALREADY BITING MY FINGERS and I'm tipsy with adrenalin. The audience is eight minutes away and I'm standing half-concealed by a holly tree. A mist is rising from the ground. Across the railway bridge, Canary Wharf explodes its podded fruit every three seconds. Out in the darkness green parakeets shriek. John (Cyclops 2) moves towards the graves on the other side of the path, to assume his position for the start of the show. "Break a leg," he says — which would be getting off lightly here. He wades into an impenetrable mass of stone and broken wood. I look through the trees. Nick is floodlit in a welter of graves, but instead of raising his viola to his chin he's sucking on an inhaler. James Trevelyan — our man on the ground — heads back to the Southern Grove entrance to give Tom the sign that the audience is on its way. Silence falls in the way I've only heard it before a performance. Adrenalin static. The last showdown with the self. Heart beatboxing in the ears.

Behind me are graves with the surname PAUL. This was my father's name, and the name we gave — in its eastern European variation — to my son, Pavel. I take this as a good luck omen. A bat circles above me, coursing a frenetic holding pattern. James sprays dry ice around Nick's position; the fake mist disperses into the thicker, genuine mist that's rising from the broken stones on the ground.

For some reason it's the poet Howard I think of now. Perhaps it's being out here, under a dark winter sky, exposed to the frosted air, that brings to mind the trenches of northern France. There's something sniffing in the brambles behind me and I turn to look: fox, nuzzling for snails. I hear a rubbing sound. It's Nick, rubbing his hands together so he's warm enough to play the viola. I flash a light across the grave I'm next to: SAMUEL KING. When I was making my way across London earlier today, from Euston to Mile End, my bag accidentally bumped the shoulder of a stranger. One of hundreds I passed. The graves here are like men of the crowd: *of* it, but in their singularity, apart. We often pass the dead without acknowledgement. This is why I'm here, to bring the living audience to meet the dead poets of Tower Hamlets Cemetery Park. I'm nervous in the way I've felt nervous

when introducing two friends from different spheres of my life. I want tonight to come off well for both parties.

I visualise where the audience will be at this point. They will have left the gates of the Southern Grove, where Tom will have given them a badge with a visual poem I've made for the occasion: 'To seek the ghost and thereby to wrap it / to wrap the ghost and thereby to seek it'. I've come to think of poetry as the ghost I carry about in my head, the words of the dead that continue to frequent my thinking as I walk through the city. What ghosts of their own will the audience bring into this space? The cemetery is always a trigger for personal loss.

We wait. Then I see the swinging orbs of torches, and hear the faint scratching of feet on the Southern Grove path. Adrenalin trip-switches my pulse; it's like the moment in the 1931 movie of *Frankenstein* when the torch-wielding mob come for him. And just like Frankenstein's monster I feel physically composed of the different parts of dead poets I've been able to find. For tonight, I've created a body of disparate texts that I'll climb inside and bring to life. There is more at stake this evening; this isn't just about my reputation, but the reputations of Herbert Ernest Howard, William Sherrard, William Ivatts, William J. Pearson, Fred Cooper, Robert Henry Bloomfield and William 'Spring' Onions. I gather them in, hold them in my mind and take a

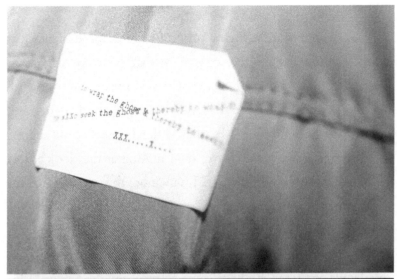

breath. Ready.

The lights are swinging towards us now, the audience just minutes away. The large electric light that James is carrying is like a lantern on a ship on a stormy night. I walk onto the path in front of them. I notice their different ages, the laughter and sadness lines around their eyes, their different heights and shapes. The white steam of breath leaves their mouths as they look at me. Floodlights wash across my face. I remember they are meeting me for the first time: the Cyclops who will lead them out across the cemetery.

I hold the moment so I can remember it later, taking in the details of those who have come to meet my dead poets. One of them looks like the actor Steven Berkoff. An elderly woman is being helped along the path by a younger woman, maybe a grand-daughter. An unshaven but smartly dressed man is wearing a long beige overcoat over his suit. Someone I can't see has brought a persistent cough. Someone I think I know, a poet, is here to join this swansong for the dead. There's also an eager man with a white beard, who doesn't want to be a part of the group, choosing instead to get as close to the performers as he can. He stands right up against me, looking into my mouth, as if my first word will come out as a moth and he'll be able to net it. They pause, waiting in life for news of the dead.

HARPREET KALSI

CYCLOPS 2: Well?

CYCLOPS 1: Well what?

CYCLOPS 2: Where *to* next?

CYCLOPS 1: Don't rush me.

CYCLOPS 2: How long do you need?

CYCLOPS 1: Before?

CYCLOPS 2: Before we go to the next place.

CYCLOPS 1: It isn't far.


As we walk towards Pearson's grave, Nick is playing the viola tenderly and with mourning, as if bringing something back to life, listening for it to speak in his ear. The grave is lit from behind. I walk towards it as the audience watches from the path. I shine a torch down on my shoes to navigate between the broken edges of graves and stones. It has taken me years to get here, years of walking, researching, documenting, and it is for this moment I did it: the audience watching this encounter between the living and the dead. Through the sound of the viola I hear a Cockney voice coming from the soundscape: "I 'ave such fury inside me". This could be the voice of the young Pearson, who had gone astray before joining the fold of the Salvation Army. I stand over the

HARPREET KALSI

dwarfed tablet of his headstone, dig in my pocket for petals, and let them fall. Deep red flakes against the matted mud of the earth. I repeat the petals, then again, like a furious shedding of the self for a poet I never knew.

Tom leads the audience off the track and into the dark, where they sit on sawn-off tree stumps. John and I enter the impromptu performance space. We are gathered in a circle, as if to witness a spirit we're about to raise.

CYCLOPS 1: It was the criminality that made him a poet.
CYCLOPS 2: How's that then?
CYCLOPS 1: Have you read Marx?
CYCLOPS 2: …Yes…
CYCLOPS 1: Those listed in the lumpenproletariat: Vagabonds, swindlers, confidence tricksters…
CYCLOPS 2: Pickpockets.
CYCLOPS 1: Gamblers, brothel-keepers, porters.
CYCLOPS 2: Bankers.
CYCLOPS 1: Bankers?
CYCLOPS 2: Sorry, *beggars*.
CYCLOPS 1: Knife-grinders, tinkers …
CYCLOPS 2: 'the whole indeterminate, fragmented mass, tossed backwards and forwards'…

CYCLOPS 1: Out at sea with the poets. The poet gave them consciousness.

CYCLOPS 2: [over-emphasises rhyme]: *La bohème in Stepney Green…*

CYCLOPS 1: Onions is the François Villon of the East End.

CYCLOPS 2: What about that time with Inspector McCarthy? There wasn't much poetry there…

CYCLOPS 1: Go on.

CYCLOPS 2: [check notes] *At one o'clock Inspector McCarthy visited him in his cell, and noticed that the walls had been scandalously defaced. He spoke to the prisoner about it, on which Onion rushed at him and struck him a violent blow on the lip, cutting it; he then struck him in the face and, catching one of his fingers between his teeth, bit it severely. It took several men to overcome him and put the handcuffs on.*

CYCLOPS 1: They were out to get him.

CYCLOPS 2: Let's just stick to the facts. Let them decide [gestures to audience].

Then we're off again, the audience following a path where the soundscape is playing back another version of the words they've just heard. Then they hear the words that are on their badges. John and I walk in a different direction; we have to get to our positions for the finale. The hours of rehearsals are now bearing fruit. Silences carry the weight of granite. Then something unscripted happens. A man who's out in the cemetery alone, and not part of the event, wants to stop and shake hands with us. Can't stop: dead poets.

At the Southern Grove entrance, the streetlights are disorientating after being in the dark cover of the cemetery for so long. They give a dream-like, sepia-tinted filter to the performance, as if we've collectively dreamt it and are now waking into reality. John reads the Howard poem at the war memorial. Nick appears and plays for the final time. Then the inevitable happens. Just as I'm about to read the last poem, a young man flies past on his bike, shocked by the audience he's momentarily surrounded by. I realise then that what I'd hoped would happen *has* happened. The audience, the performers and the dead have become one. We have merged into a single artifice. The boundaries between life and death — and life and performance — have dissolved.

We have walked through darkness with the dead. The lost poets have been heard. We will take their words with us, amplified to London's endless night.

# ACKNOWLEDGEMENTS

I am hugely grateful to Arts Council England for awarding me Grants for the Arts funding to allow me to write this book.

Thanks to Ken Greenway, cemetery manager at Tower Hamlets Cemetery Park, for supporting this project, for making time to walk with me in the grounds of the cemetery and for collaborating on organising the series of performances in November 2016 and October 2019. Diane Kendall has been an invaluable guide, providing the first links to many of the poets documented in this book. I would like to credit Joyce Cracknell for her research on William 'Spring' Onions. Thanks also to the Trustees and Friends of Tower Hamlets Cemetery Park.

Thanks to Angela Underhill for responding to my letter to the Robert Bloomfield Society. Many thanks to Professor John Goodridge for helping to solve the mystery of 'The Poet Bloomfield' and for giving such invaluable background on the life and work of Robert Bloomfield.

A huge thanks to Stephen Watts for agreeing to walk with me in the cemetery, for sharing his knowledge and for responding with his poem 'Lost Poets My East End' which is included in this book.

Thanks to Spitalfields Festival for commissioning the Dead Poets Social Club performances in Tower Hamlets Cemetery Park in 2016, and to Tom Chivers, James Trevelyan, John Canfield and Nick Murray for appearing in them. Thanks to Harpreet Kalsi for his photographs, many of which are used in this book.

I would like to thank my wife Sarah Crewe for allowing me to bring the dead poets of Tower Hamlets Cemetery Park into our lives and helping to work out the life of Robert Henry Bloomfield. And thank you to my son Pavel for always pulling me out of the rabbit hole of dead poets.

Finally, a big thanks as always to my editor Tom Chivers: for encouragement, insight and pushing to bring out the best in my writing.

SELECTED BIBLIOGRAPHY

Guillaume Apollinaire, *Selected Poems*, translated by Oliver Bernard, London: Anvil Press Poetry, 1986

Catherine Arnold, *Necropolis: London and its Dead*, London: Simon & Schuster, 2007

Cyril J. Barnes, *He Conquered the Foe: William J. Pearson*, London: Salvationist Publishing and Supplies, 1956

Matthew Beaumont, *Nightwalking: A Nocturnal History of London*, London: Verso Books, 2015

Robert Bloomfield, *Selected Poems: Revised and Enlarged Edition*, edited by John Goodridge and John Lucas, Nottingham: Trent Editions, 2007

Robert Bolano, *2666*, translated by Natasha Wimmer, London: Picador, 2009

Roger Bowdler, *Tower Hamlets Cemetery, Southern Grove, London E3: Historic and Conservation Report*; English Heritage, Historic & Research Team, Reports and Papers 5, 1999

Chris Brooks, *Mortal Remains: The History and Present State of the Victorian and Edwardian Cemetery*, Exeter: Wheaton, in association with The Victorian Society, 1989

Thomas Burke, *Out and About London*, New York: Henry Holt and Company, 1919

Brian Catling, *The Vorrh: Book One in the Vorrh Trilogy*, London: Coronet, 2016

Robert Desnos, *Surrealist, Lover, Resistant: Collected Poems*, translated by

Timothy Ades, Todmorden: Arc, 2017

Charles Dickens, *A Christmas Carol and Other Christmas Stories*, Oxford: Oxford University Press, 2008

Charles Dickens. 'Night Walks' from *The Uncommercial Traveller*, introduced by Peter Ackroyd, London: Mandarin, 1991

Alfred Doblin, *Berlin Alexanderplatz*, translated by Michael Hoffman, London: Penguin Classics, 2018

Friedrich Engels, *The Condition of the Working Class in England*, Oxford: Oxford University Press, 1993

John Felstiner, *Paul Celan: Poet, Survivor, Jew*, New Haven and London: Yale University Press, 2001

James Greenwood, *In Strange Company: Being the Experiences of a Roving Correspondent*, Goring-by-Sea, Dodo Press, 2009

Isabella M. Holmes, *The London Burial Grounds: Notes on their History from the Earliest Times to the Present Day*, London, 1896; reprinted by Amazon in the Odins Library Classic series

Barbara Jones, *Design for Death*, London: Andre Deutsch, 1967

Jack London, *The People of the Abyss*, Tangerine Press in Association with L-13 Light Industrial Workshop, 2014 (originally published 1903)

Henry Mayhew, *London Labour and the London Poor*, Oxford: Oxford University Press, 2012

Hugh Meller and Brian Parsons, *London Cemeteries: An Illustrated Guide and Gazetteer*, Amersham: Avebury Publishing Company, 2011

William Morris, *A Dream of John Ball*, New York: Oriole Chapbooks, (reprint of 1887 edition)

Thomas Nashe, *The Terrors of the Night*, London: Penguin Books, 2015

Christopher Ricks, *The New Oxford Book of Victorian Verse*, Oxford: Oxford University Press, 1990

Isaac Rosenberg, *The Collected Poems*, London: Chatto & Windus, 1974

Chris Searle (editor), *Bricklight: Poems from the Labour Movement in East London*, London: Pluto Press in association with The National Museum of Labour History, 1980

W.G. Sebald, *Austerlitz*, translated by Anthea Bell, London: Hamish Hamilton, 2001

William Shakespeare, *Anthony and Cleopatra*, Oxford: Oxford University Press, 2008

William Shakespeare, *Julius Caesar*, Oxford: Oxford University Press, 2001

James Thomson (B.V.), *The City of Dreadful Night*, introduced by Edwin Morgan, Edinburgh: Canongate Classics, 1993

James Thomson (B.V.), *The Complete Poems*, edited by A.J. Spatz, Arlington VA: Charles & Wonder, 2012

John Turpin & Derrick Knight, *The Magnificent Seven: London's First Landscaped Cemeteries*, Gloucesterhsire: Aberley Books, 2011

Louis Untermeyer (editor), *The Albatross Book of Living Verse: English and American Poetry from the Thirteenth Century to the Present Day*, London: Collins Publishers, 1933

Stephen Watts, *Ancient Sunlight*, London: Enitharmon Press, 2014

Stephen Watts, *The Blue Bag*, London, Delhi, Ontario: AARK ARTS, 2004

Stephen Watts, *Republic of Dogs / Republic of Birds*, London: Test Centre, 2016

ONLINE RESOURCES

Figures on London population taken from https://www.victorianlondon.org/
population/population.htm and https://www.trustforlondon.org.uk/data/
londons-population-over-time/

Robert Henry Bloomfield, 'The Musical World' 36-37, vol. xix, September
5-12 1844, available on Google Books

The British Newspaper Archive has been an essential source for accounts of
the dead poets: https://www.britishnewspaperarchive.co.uk/

Herbert Ernest Howard, *Verses from the Trenches: "The Charge" and Other
Poems*, 1916, found at www.bl.uk/collection-items/verses-from-the-
trenches

Background on Tower Hamlets Cemetery Park: https://londonist.com/
london/secret/things-you-didn-t-know-about-tower-hamlets-cemetery

William 'Spring' Onions reports on Jack the Ripper tour website https://
www.jack-the-ripper-tour.com/generalnews/william-onions-the-east-end-
poet/

William Morris, 'A Death Song', found at University of Maryland Digital
Collections, https://digital.lib.umd.edu/image?pid=umd:96541

Salvation Army, *The Song Book of the Salvation Army*, New York: Territorial
Headquarters, 1953. Available online at https://hymnary.org/hymnal/
SBSA1953

# INDEX